The Internet & Web Design for Teachers

A STEP-BY-STEP GUIDE TO CREATING A VIRTUAL CLASSROOM

The Internet & Web Design for Teachers

A STEP-BY-STEP GUIDE TO CREATING A VIRTUAL CLASSROOM

DENNIS ANDERSON, PH.D.

Pace University

Longman

New York   San Francisco   Boston
London   Toronto   Sydney   Singapore   Madrid
Mexico City   Munich   Paris   Cape Town   Hong Kong   Montreal

Acquisitions Editor: Aurora Martinez Ramos
Marketing Manager: Kathleen Morgan
Production Coordinator: Shafiena Ghani
Design Manager and Technical Desktop Manager: Heather A. Peres
Cover Design Manager: Wendy Ann Fredericks
Cover Photo: ©Jim Starr/Stockart.com
Manufacturing Buyer: Al Dorsey
Electronic Page Makeup: Heather A. Peres
Printer and Binder: Courier
Cover Printer: Lehigh Press, Inc.

For permission to use copyrighted material, grateful acknowledgment is made to the copyright holders on pp. 107 – 114, which are hereby made part of this copyright page.

Library of Congress Cataloging-in-Publication Data

Anderson, Dennis, Ph.D.
    The Internet & Web design for teachers: a step-by-step guide to creating a virtual classroom./Dennis Anderson.
        p. cm.
    ISBN 0-321-07751-2
 1. Internet in education. 2. Web sites—Design. I. Title: Internet and Web design for teachers. II. Title.

LB1044.87 A53 2001
025.04'024'372—dc21

                                                                    00-049736

Copyright © 2001 by Addison-Wesley Educational Publishers Inc.

The information in this book is subject to change without notice and the author and publisher assume no responsibility for error or omissions. The author and publisher assume no reponsibility for any Web site, program, and product mentioned in this book. All Web sites mentioned in this book belong to the rightful owners of the Web site.

Please visit our website at *http://www.ablongman.com*

ISBN 0-321-07751-2

12345678910—CRS—03020100

To every teacher who is dedicated
to lifelong learning

Docendo discimus
"By teaching, we learn"

Contents

Preface ix

CHAPTER 1 INTRODUCTION   1

CHAPTER 2 THE INTERNET AND WORLD WIDE WEB   5

PART A ✳ **INTERNET SOURCES, SAMPLES, AND WEB RESOURCES**   13

CHAPTER 3 A SURVEY OF INTERNET TECHNOLOGIES USEFUL TO EDUCATORS   15

    A) E-mail   16
    B) Online Chat   22
    C) Video and Audio Conferencing and Streaming   22
    D) Listservs and Newsgroups   23

CHAPTER 4 USING SEARCH ENGINES AND WEB BROWSERS: HOW TO FIND EVERYTHING YOU AND YOUR STUDENTS NEED   27

CHAPTER 5 A CRITICAL CATALOGUE OF USEFUL WEB SITES FOR TEACHERS   33

    1) Science   34
    2) Mathematics   42
    3) Social Studies   45

4) English, Literature, and Writing-Related
    Web Sites   47
5) Foreign Languages   49
6) Physical Education and Health   51
7) Art and Music   52
8) Vocational Education   55

PART B ✳ INTERNET-BASED CURRICULUM DESIGN   57

CHAPTER 6 BUILDING A WEB SITE   59

Off-the-Shelf Web-Editor Software   60
Customizing Your Own Web Page with HTML   62
A) Hyperlinks   76
B) Downloading Images and Texts   77
C) Electronic Tables and Forms   79
D) Telnet and FTP   87

CHAPTER 7 ADVANCED LESSONS   89

A) Creating Virtual Classrooms   89
B) Other Recommendations   89

APPENDIX: EDUCATION-RELATED LISTSERVS   97

GLOSSARY   105

Preface

As developing technologies change the world around us, educators are trying to find ways to adapt their teaching styles to a more complex world. In just the past three decades computers have evolved from simple number crunchers to word processors to gateways to the unlimited resources made available through the Internet. I cannot recall any other technology that changed so fast and had so much impact on society in such a short time period. The World Wide Web now allows us to do things that educators used only to dream about, giving us access to a nearly infinite amount of information and enabling us to organize it and present it through engaging multimedia presentations. These changes are daunting, yet also encouraging and exciting. Teachers have started reexamining their mission and goals in light of the opportunities that these new technologies present.

All across the country classrooms are being wired for Internet access. But few teachers have the experience, knowledge, and training necessary to turn this great technological leap into a lasting benefit for their students. It may be painful, but teachers can no longer think of themselves as the center of knowledge. They must become learners, like their students. While computers are essential to this new technology, they are just an aid, not a replacement for a skilled and caring teacher. (Those who worry about computers replacing warm-blooded humans can rest easy.) Just as technology provides more learning options for students, so we have to learn how to use technologies to make us more confident and effective as teachers.

This book aims to give K–12 teachers the tools they need to take advantage of the educational opportunities provided by the Internet and the World Wide Web. It is part catalogue--with a comprehensive listing and critique of Web sites of use to K–12 teachers--and part how-to guide for teachers who want to create their own cyber classrooms.

Today's teachers are explorers, information gatherers, and facilitators, helping students master the skills they will need to access a new world of knowledge. I hope this book can benefit those pioneers who do not mind getting their feet wet to better our educational system.

Please address all comments and questions to the author:

Dennis Anderson, Ph.D., M.Phil., Ed.M., M.S.
School of Computer Science and Information Systems
Pace University
1 Pace Plaza
New York, NY 10038

http://www.csis.pace.edu/~anderson
danderson@pace.edu

The Internet & Web Design for Teachers

A STEP-BY-STEP GUIDE TO CREATING A VIRTUAL CLASSROOM

Introduction

That's one small step for man, one giant leap for mankind.

◆ *Neil Armstrong*

PURPOSE

Recent advances in telecommunications and computer technology, especially the Internet, have transformed everything from banking to book buying to making plane reservations. This cyber revolution is now coming to classrooms across the United States, giving educators powerful new tools to advance teaching and learning. The Internet and World Wide Web provide instant access to an almost unlimited trove of information and images and make possible interactions among students, parents, and teachers around the world. American high-school students have chatted online with their counterparts in Bosnia about the troubles in the Balkans. Others have taken virtual field trips to the Louvre art museum and the Amazon.

This book is written for K–12 teachers and college-level instructors who want to use Internet technologies to enrich the quality of learning in their classrooms. Thanks to grants from the government and private foundations, more and more schools are being wired for Internet access. But few teachers are receiving the training they need to put this resource to work for their students. The aim of this book is to help bridge that knowledge gap. It is part catalogue, with a comprehensive listing and critique of Web sites useful for K–12 teachers, and part how-to guide for teachers who want to create their own cyber classrooms. The book will take you, step-by-step and with a minimum of technical buzz words, through the process of creating Web pages–and even entire virtual schools. (Most of

1

the technical terms that are used are in bold-faced type and included in the glossary at the end of the book.)

Adopting these technologies will allow you to pick and choose educational resources from around the globe for use in your classes. You will be able to communicate with your colleagues, students, and parents in new and innovative ways. There are infinite options and your creativity is only the limit. But these changes will also necessitate changes in the way you teach, since you will no longer be the only center of information. More than ever before, today's teachers are becoming explorers, information gatherers, and facilitators who help students master skills and acquire knowledge.

It is important, however, not to get carried away by the bells and whistles offered by new technology. The resources of the Internet and World Wide Web are most effective when they are part of a well-thought-out and focused teaching strategy. Use technology to support your teaching goals. Do not allow it to dictate what and how you teach.

Before you can start using the Internet in your teaching, you need to do a survey of your school's computer facilities and budget. First of all, you need to find out if your school is wired for Internet access. Do you have computers in your classroom? Does your classroom have a high-speed data connection? Does the school have a computer lab? And is it connected to the Internet? You also need to find out if your school has its own Internet server. An Internet server is a specialized computer that stores Web sites, electronic mail, and provides other important Internet services. You should also do a quick inventory to see if your school has other useful accessories such as a digital camera, photo scanner, audio and video equipment, and various software programs.

To use the Internet in your classroom teaching, you'll need at least one **multimedia computer** with a high-speed Pentium chip and a **modem.** Many Internet-ready computers come with a modem already installed. This allows your PC to communicate with other computers using telephone lines. If your computer doesn't already have a modem, you should buy one that can transmit at least 56 kilobytes per second. If your school is not already wired, once your computer is ready, it is time to shop for an **Internet Service Provider.** There are hundreds of ISPs to choose from, and all can serve as your gateway to the World Wide Web.

If your school is already wired, you probably have two main choices open to you: You can either teach in a computer lab or a classroom with multimedia computers connected to the Internet. There are pros and cons to both. A computer lab, provided it has enough workstations, can give all students a hands-on experience, heightening their experience of autonomy and self-discovery. In this setup, a teacher is a facilitator. So, before going into the lab, you might want to read up on group learning, active learning, and cooperative learning. The downside of a computer lab is that if you don't execute your plan carefully, you can end up with 20 students doing 20 different things. Labs also are not immune to technical problems—such as network crashes or printer failures—that can eat up valuable class time.

A single Internet-ready multimedia computer in a classroom offers a teacher more control. The computer should be able to handle large amounts of data at a fast rate. Any of today's high-speed Pentium computers would be adequate. The classroom would also have to be wired to provide a fast network speed. In this arrangement, students don't participate as directly as they do in a lab. Technology can also fail you, but in your own classroom, it may be easier to switch to your backup lesson plan if things don't work out.

If your school system needs help paying for computer equipment, there are a wide variety of funding sources available, both public and private. With the economy booming, many corporations are willing to lend a hand. Lists of grant-giving foundations are easy to find on the Internet or in public libraries.

The Internet and World Wide Web

By now, even if you have never used the Internet, you no doubt have heard much about it and the World Wide Web from movies and television. Often they are portrayed as hard-to-understand and intimidating. Don't worry. The Internet and World Wide Web are not nearly as foreign as they sound. And computer scientists have already done most of the heavy lifting required to make these technologies easy to use, even for the inexperienced.

The Internet is a global network of computers interconnected so they can share data and resources. This network is, ironically, a product of the Cold War designed to defend the nation from the threat of a Soviet nuclear attack. In the late 1960s, the U.S. Department of Defense created a network of computers to share military data in case of such an attack. This ingenious project, known as ARPANET (Advanced Research Project Agency Network), was the beginning of the Internet. Soon, the network was extended to scientists, educators, and other public organizations. And in the early 1990s, the network was opened to commercial organizations as well.

The Internet is now accessible anytime, anywhere for people with computers that can connect to the network. And it is growing rapidly. There are now about 56 million host computers connected to the Internet. *Nielsen Media Research* and *NetRatings* estimate that in 1999, there were

35 million U.S. households, or about 98.9 million people, with Internet access. That's more than a third of all Americans. Around the world, about 215 million people are connected to the Internet, according to Global Reach.

Much of the Internet's content these days is organized as pages on the World Wide Web. The Web is a service that allows people to exchange electronic documents and data using the same graphical interface. It was introduced by Tim-Burners Lee in 1992, and makes it possible to include text, pictures, video images, animation, and sound. The Web communicates with all these types of data by using hyperlinks, or virtual connections between documents.

To view Web content, you must use software known as a **Web browser.** Web browsers can be obtained easily from a number of sources. Today there are two major Web browsers competing in the market, Microsoft Internet Explorer and Netscape Communicator. If you are online, you can check out Netscape at *www.netscape.com.* To find Internet Explorer, visit *www.microsoft.com.*

These two can be downloaded from the Internet free of charge or purchased on a CD from a local software store. Netscape and Internet Explorer are not completely compatible, and some Web pages work better on one than the other. Navigating the Web with the help of these browsers, users can view pages with a few clicks of the mouse. All you need to know is a site's address. In Web-speak, the address is known as an **URL,** short for **Uniform Resource Locator.** Typing the URL into the so-called location box on your browser will take you to the Web page you desire.

Web pages themselves are fairly easy to create, even for lay people. Odds are at least some of your students have already posted Web sites of their own. To build a Web site, you use a simple computer language known as **Hypertext Markup Language** or **HTML.** Software known as "Web editor" programs is included with many Web browsers and can be used to create simple Web pages. More advanced Web-page design programs can be purchased or downloaded free from the Internet.

Figure 2-1. As you can see, Web sites look different when viewed using different Web browsers. Here's what my home page looks like viewed with Microsoft Internet Explorer (IE).

The Internet is capable of carrying all kinds of multimedia data, including video and audio streams.

FIGURE 2-1

◆ *Microsoft Internet (IE).*

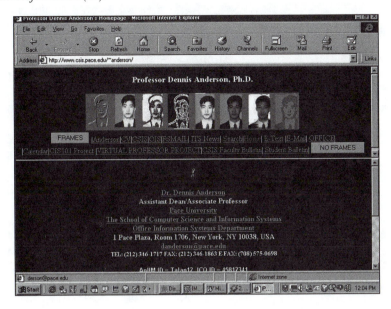

FIGURE 2-2

◆ *Here's what it looks like using Netscape Navigator.*

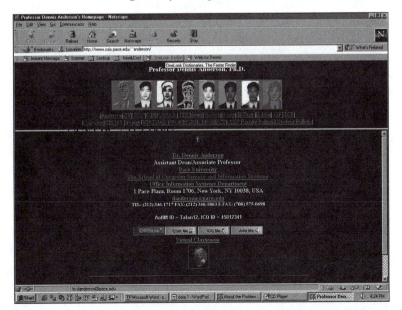

FIGURE 2-3

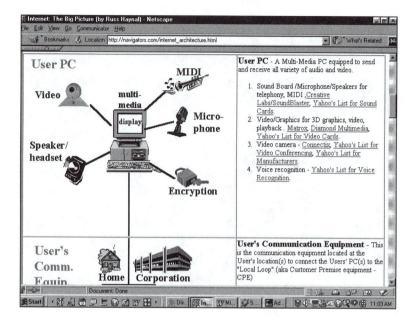

FIGURE 2-4

◆ *In order to connect to the Internet, a computer needs a device such as a modem. Modems convert a computer's digital signal into an analog signal that can travel over telephone lines and vice versa. Computers hooked to a local-area network, or LAN, use a network card to communicate with other computers.*

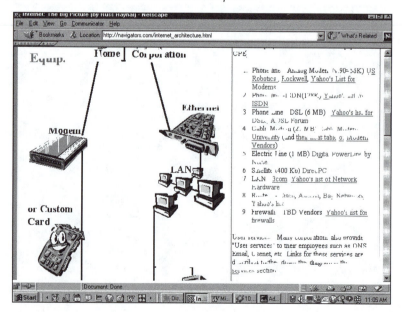

FIGURE 2-5

◆ *A firewall provides security from unauthorized access to an internal network.*

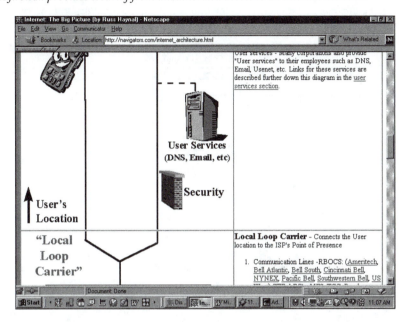

FIGURE 2-6

◆ *Data can be transmitted over coaxial cable, copper, or fiber-optic telephone lines, and be beamed through the air by wireless transmissions.*

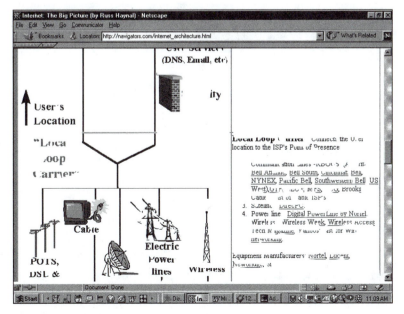

FIGURE 2-7

◆ *To connect to the Internet, you must have an Internet Service Provider, or ISP, a company that makes a connection to the Internet. An account with a local ISP typically costs less then $20 per month, depending on what features you want.*

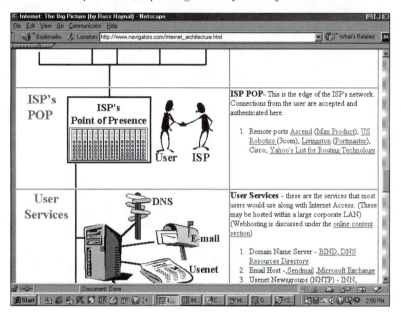

FIGURE 2-8

◆ *Your ISP connects you to the rest of the Internet community.*

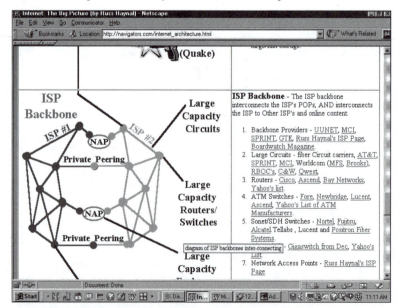

FIGURE 2-9

◆ *Host computers provide Internet contents.*

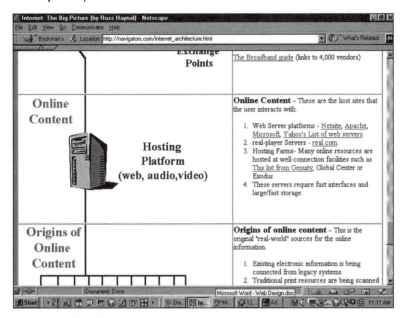

FIGURE 2-10

◆ *Host computers maintain all kinds of materials that have been stored so that other people can access them at any time from anywhere.*

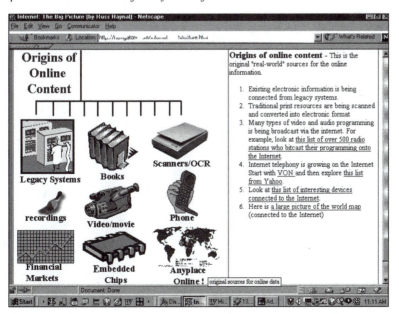

Part A

Internet Sources, Samples, and Web Resources

A Survey of Internet Technologies Useful to Educators

In this chapter, we will explore a number of common Internet technologies that are especially useful for teachers. As you will see, there are many options open to you, all of which can be used to create course activities that encourage active learning and collaboration. Your challenge is to choose the technologies that are most suitable for your students and that are best geared to advance your teaching goals. For example, online chat is a powerful tool, but might not be a good choice for younger students. Letting your students loose on the Internet also limits your ability to control what information they can access. In some cases, special screens that limit access to undesirable content, such as pornography, may be necessary. To maximize benefits, it is strongly recommended that you integrate technologies into your teaching plans with very specific educational aims. This chapter will provide a brief description of Internet technologies including **e-mail**, **telnet**, **ftp**, video and audio conferencing and streaming, Listservs, and newsgroups.

A) E-MAIL

E-mail is the most common and widely used Internet technology. It allows nearly instantaneous written communication and also allows users to send data, computer programs, pictures, video, and audio recordings. E-mail can be a useful way to connect with your colleagues, answer students' questions, and get in touch with working parents. Some teachers encourage students to submit homework via e-mail and use it to offer after-school online help.

Introducing students to e-mail also provides an opportunity to teach proper online behavior, or what the denizens of cyber-space call netiquette. Netiquette encourages people to use the same standards in electronic communications that they would use in written letters and polite face-to-face interactions. There are a number of Web sites dedicated to netiquette, which offer pointers for good manners in the use of e-mail, newsgroups, and chat rooms. Five of the best are:

- *http://www.hamil.demon.co.uk/conf/nettiq.htm,* which discusses general netiquette.
- *http://cheeky.dsl.psn.net/~ircadmin/grnet/nettiq.html,* with pointers on how to behave in chat rooms.
- *http://www.wpi.edu/Help/Internet/nettiq.html,* specializes in netiquette for e-mail, mailing lists, and newsgroups.
- *http://www.albion.com/netiquette/corerules.html,* with the core rules of netiquette.
- *http://jade.wabash.edu/wabnet/info/netiquet.htm,* which provides a good introduction to network etiquette.

You and your students can obtain a free e-mail account on the Internet by visiting one of free e-mail giveaway Web sites such as Microsoft's hotmail (*www.hotmail.com*), or Yahoo (*www.yahoo.com*). Many other Internet portal sites also offer free e-mail as an enticement to get consumers to visit their sites. These free e-mail accounts are accessible from anywhere you have access to the Internet—and you do not have to download any software. If your school has a server, individual e-mail accounts also may be obtained from your school's computer-system administrator. And many Internet Service Providers, such as AOL or Mindspring, offer e-mail as part of a package of services.

The way e-mail works provides an excellent primer on the way the entire Internet functions. Let's look at how e-mail works step by step.

Sender: (You should be connected already to your ISP.)

1. Open an e-mail program to compose an e-mail on your PC. There are more than thirty-one e-mail programs, including Eudora Pro,

FIGURE 3-1

◆ *Yahoo.com is one of many sites that provide free e-mail accounts.*

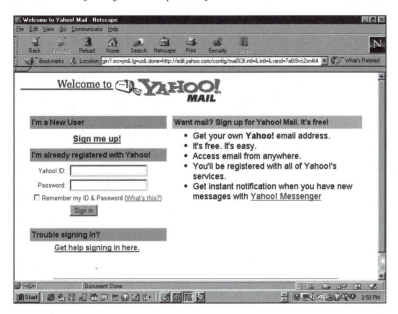

FIGURE 3-2

◆ *You can find an online e-mail guide at www.alabanza.com/kabacoff/ Inter-Links/email/email.html. This Web site provides a nice summary of what e-mail service is all about.*

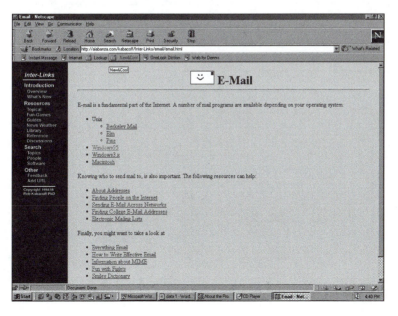

Outlook Express, and Pegasus. Many Web browsers also include e-mail programs. Before you can use the e-mail program, you must configure the settings under Web browser's PREFERENCES option. It is best you consult with your Internet Service Provider for this information.

2. Most likely, your e-mail program has user-friendly navigation buttons on the menu bar at the top of the screen. You should see self-explanatory buttons such as Compose, Send, Receive, and Attach.

3. Choose or click on the Compose option.

4. Type in the e-mail address of the receiver. An e-mail address is composed of a user name, a computer-domain name, and an "at" sign, the now ubiquitous @, in between. For example, my e-mail address is *danderson@csis.pace.edu*. That represents user Dennis Anderson at the School of Computer Science and Information Systems at Pace University. Edu is a domain name commonly used for educational institutions in the United States.

FIGURE 3-3

◆ *Sample e-mail screen in Netscape has common menu items such as new message or compose, get messages, reply, forward, and print.*

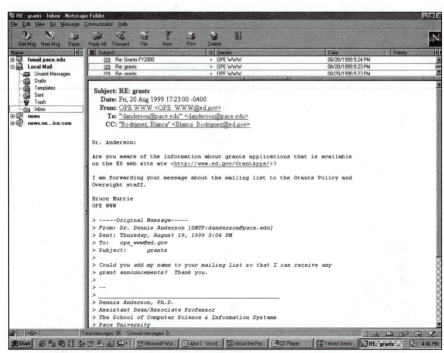

DOMAIN NAMES

Domain names specify the physical location of information on the Internet. Web domains are the same as the e-mail domains. There are a few domain-name suffixes that are useful to know. For example, someone who works for the *Wall Street Journal* might have a company Web address *http://www.wsj.com* and an e-mail address of *someone@wsj.com*.

- EDU: educational site, i.e., *www.mit.edu, www.pace.edu*
- COM: commercial site, i.e., *www.ibm.com, www.amazon.com*
- GOV: government site, i.e., *www.loc.gov, www.whitehouse.gov*
- ORG: nonprofit organization site, i.e., *www.clir.org, www.metmuseum.org*
- NET: net or commercial Web site, i.e., *designet.vi.net*
- Web domains in foreign countries often have a two-letter country designation, such as "uk" for the United Kingdom, "kr" for Korea or "th" for Thailand. Here are some overseas Web addresses: *www.open.ac.uk, www.bcs.org.uk, www.dong-a-ilbo.co.kr.* It is important to note, however, that not all foreign Web addresses have a country indicator at the end of the address.
- Some U.S. Web sites, especially local government Web sites, have the two letter domain name "us" at the end of the Web address, i.e., *www.mta.nyc.ny.us.*

Most e-mail programs allow you to send carbon copies to other users, just as you would with a paper memo. It is a common courtesy to fill in the Subject line so that the receiver can see what your e-mail is about before actually opening the message.

5. Compose your e-mail in the body.
6. You can also attach a file such as a document, picture, or sound. There is often a limit to the size of the files you can attach to an e-mail. Usually, you cannot attach a file larger than 2 mega-bytes. That still allows you to send plenty of information, however. Two mega-bytes is about the size of two full floppy disks. To attach a file, simply click on the "attachments" icon. This will then allow you to select a file from those saved on your computer and send it along with your e-mail.
7. When you are done, click on the Send option.

Receiver: (You should be already connected to your ISP.)

1. Open your e-mail program.
2. If you have e-mail, your e-mail program often will automatically retrieve messages from the ISP's server. If not, you may have to click on the Receive option to download your messages.

3. You can click on the message heading to read your message.

4. If you want to reply to the message, you can choose the Reply option. Depending on your e-mail program's set-up, the sender's original message may be included automatically at the bottom of your response.

5. When you finish composing your reply, you can click on the Send option to dispatch your message.

6. If there is an attachment to the e-mail, you can click on it to either open it or save it for later use. It is important not to open strange or unexpected attachments, since they can contain extremely disruptive computer viruses. There are a few new viruses that even attach themselves to messages without the sender's knowledge. This was the case with Melissa virus, which spread across the United States in 1999, and wreaked havoc in corporate computer systems.

7. E-mail users should also look out for "spam," the Internet equivalent of junk mail. You and your students could become the targets of unscrupulous people promoting get-rich-quick schemes, stock offerings for unknown start-up corporations, quack remedies, and illegally pirated software.

8. You can exit your program by choosing the Exit option in the menu.

FIGURE 3-4

◆ *Packet switching is the key to how all electronic transmissions take place on the Internet.*

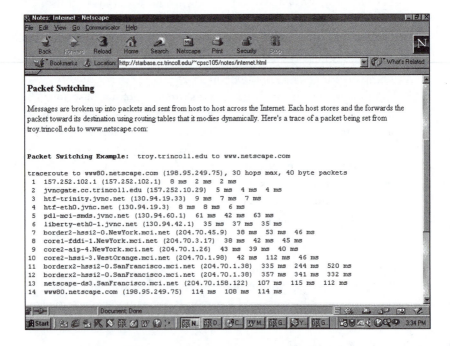

FIGURE 3-5

◆ *Example of packet switching in a Japanese network.*

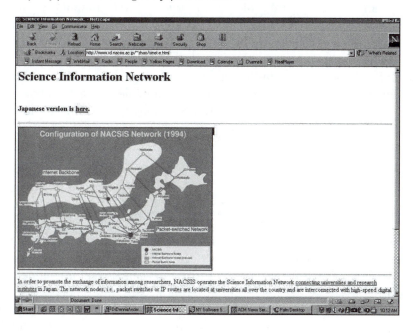

FIGURE 3-6

◆ *Sample IRC screen showing multi-users in a chat room.*

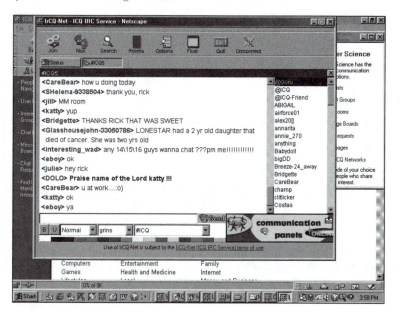

Now we know what to do to send and receive e-mail. But what happens to our messages as they travel from point A to point B? When an e-mail or any other data are sent over the Internet, the contents are broken up into tiny packets that each travel through different network channels. Each one is tagged with the address of the message's final destination. When all the packets arrive, they are reassembled in the right order. The technology that makes this possible is called packet switching. Packet switching makes Internet communication possible. It saves money and time because it allows millions of transmissions to move over the same wires at the same time, eliminating the need for expensive one-to-one connections between senders and receivers.

B) ONLINE CHAT

Online chat programs give teachers and students the opportunity to have real-time online exchanges. Teachers can use this technology to conduct after-school tutorials with students. Instructors can also set up online chats that bring together students from different classes and schools to discuss current events or other course-related topics of interest. Online chats can even allow instant interactions between students in different cities and different countries. All that is needed is the right computer program.

One common chat program is Internet Relay Chat. It can be downloaded from the Web site IRC.com. The software allows users access to IRC's chat channels and allows you to create your own discussion group or join in existing chat rooms. You can chat one-on-one or in large groups. When you are chatting, your computer screen is usually divided into two sections, one for your responses and the other for comments from the other person or people in the chat room. IRC does not provide any particular structure to ensure a constructive discussion.

There are other chat programs that allow users to create their own chat rooms. As an administrator, you can organize your own chat room with announcements and user files.

C) VIDEO AND AUDIO CONFERENCING AND STREAMING

Another tool that can create an interactive learning environment is video and audio conferencing. But technical constraints at present make this an expensive and cumbersome technology for most users these days. Unless your school has a very fast Internet connection, actually viewing a long-running video stream or conducting an online video conference can be extremely frustrating. The best classroom use of these technologies these days is to download brief video and audio clips, such as sound bites from famous speakers. In the future, however, as computers become more powerful and the network connecting them gains higher-speed transmission capacity, it will be possible to use the Internet to show documentaries and feature-length films. It should even be possible to broadcast or tape your class for students who are homesick.

D) LISTSERVS AND NEWSGROUPS

Listservs are services that distribute information via an electronic mailing list to people interested in a given topic, such as the teaching of reading. To subscribe, you must find the address of the Listserv administrator, and send a simple message or command, asking to be added to the list. In most cases, you send an e-mail without a subject heading. In the body of the message, write: "subscribe Your Name."

Once you are on the list, you will receive e-mails from other subscribers. You will be able to send e-mail to everyone on the list as well. This is a good way of sharing ideas and information with people who have similar interests.

Newsgroups are similar to Listservs, but the information you will receive comes only from the group administrator, not directly from other subscribers. Newsgroups disseminate news about specified topics to people who are interested in those topics. There are thousands of Listservs and newsgroups, many dedicated to education-related issues. The name of the Listserv generally provides information about the focus of the Listserv. You can always send an e-mail or go to the Listserv's Web site to get more information. For a list of good, education-related Listservs and newsgroups, see the Appendix.

FIGURE 3-7

◆ *Sample Listserv delivers a news item to the subscribed user.*

FIGURE 3-8

◆ *Education newsgroups.*

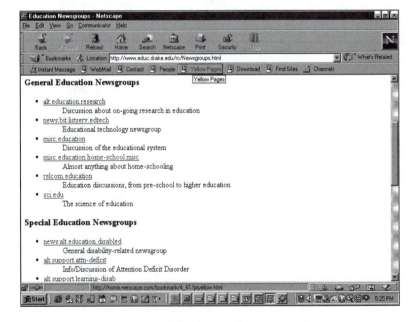

FIGURE 3-9

◆ *This sample shows how professional news is delivered online every morning to thousands of subscribers. It is almost like a morning newspaper.*

CHAPTER 4

Using Search Engines and Web Browsers: How to Find Everything You and Your Students Need

SEARCH ON THE INTERNET

Searching for information on the Internet can be a bit like prospecting for gold in the Old West. Where should you look? And how do you know if what you've found is real and not just fool's gold? These are two critical questions for teachers who want to use the Internet to find information for classes and research projects. There is a vast amount of information on the Internet, some of it contributed by scientists, academics, governments, libraries, and other reputable sources. But much of the Web's contents have been posted by the man or woman down the street, who has something to share. Increasingly, too, the Internet is becoming more commercial. A lot of the information on the Web is posted by people looking to sell you something.

To sort through the almost limitless supply of information on the Internet, you use a tool called a **search engine**. These are powerful computer programs that search the World Wide Web for sites that contain the information you are looking for. Some popular search engines are *Go.com, Netscape.com, Altavista.com, Hotbot.com, Lycos.com, Yahoo.com,* and *Excite.com.* Different search engines will often come up with different results.

Some search engines concentrate on finding people. These are basically white pages that list individuals. You can search for anyone who is listed in a local telephone book and often find out that person's telephone number, e-mail address, and home address. You can even get a map of the person's neighborhood. Another set of specialized search engines, called meta-search engines, will feed your search request into a large number of regular search engines and assemble all of the results for you. Some popular meta-search engines include: *About.com, Justseek.com, Google.com,* and *Askjeeves.com.* It is a good idea to try several and see which you like the best.

Once you have chosen a search engine, look for the box in which you can type in a few key words that describe what you are looking for. If you receive too many matches, or hits, you may want to be more specific. If you get too few hits, try to be more general in your search request. Many search engines offer advanced search tools that allow you to narrow your search by defining a phrase (words placed within quotation marks) that must appear exactly in a Web site to get a match, or to list multiple words (linked together with "and"), that all must be present to score a hit. If you are not satisfied with the outcome, you should try another search engine.

It can be easy to get sidetracked, given the huge amount of information on the Web. So it is important to stay focused. And never forget to verify that the information you discover is credible. The Internet is full of hoaxes.

Other search engines can be found at:

www.justseek.com
www.excite.com

FIGURE 4-1

◆ *Yahoo.com is one of the best-known search engines.*

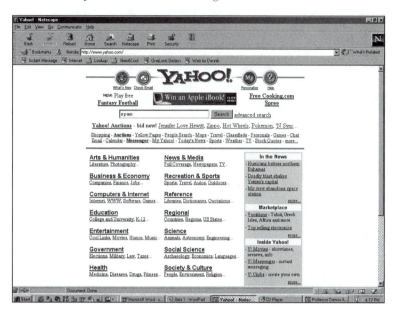

FIGURE 4-2

◆ *Altavista.com has one of the largest databases.*

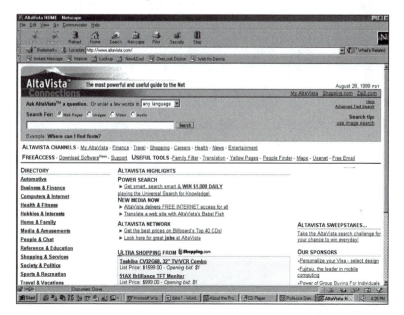

FIGURE 4-3

◆ *Hotbot.com offers free e-mail, home pages, message boards, and chat.*

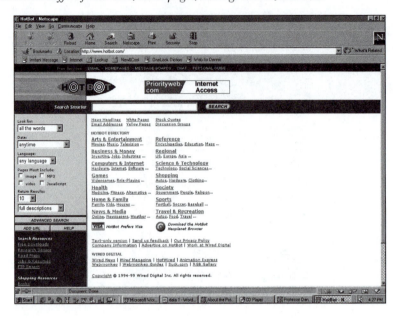

FIGURE 4-4

◆ *Switchboard.com allows you to find a person, business, e-mail, Web pages, and maps.*

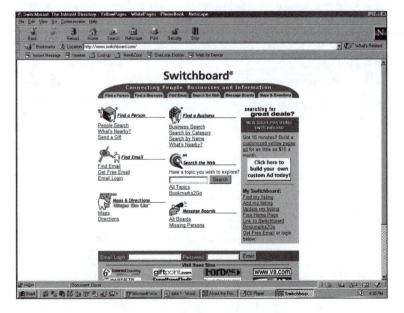

FIGURE 4-5

◆ *The Ultimate White Pages Web site provides a composite of widely used white pages.*
Anyone listed in a phone book can be found on the Internet today.

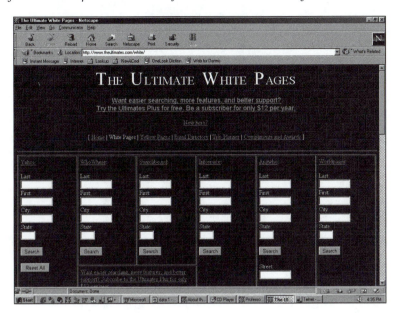

www.lycos.com
www.google.com
www.ussc.alltheweb.com
www.goto.com
www.deja.com
www.infoseek.com
www.northernlight.com
www.directhit.com
www.mamma.com
www.allonesearch.com

Some search engines specialize in specific fields. For example:

www.maths.usyd.edu.au:8000/MathSearch.html, for math-related
   topics.

musicsearch.com, for music.

w1.xrefer.com, which searches encyclopedias and other reference works.

CHAPTER 5

A Critical Catalogue of Useful Web Sites for Teachers

This chapter provides a critical catalogue of the most useful education-related Web sites for teachers. This list is always changing, as new sites are added to the Web and outdated ones are deleted. Given this wealth of information, your role as a filter and tour guide for your students is more important than ever. You should also look critically at the Web sites you plan to use in your classes. Are they accurate? Are they presenting information in a balanced way? Or do they represent just one school of thought on a subject? It is important to teach your students that they should not take what they see or hear on the Internet literally as a fact. And they should understand that the Web mirrors the diversity of opinion in the real world.

Another thing to look for in a Web site is the organization of its content. Is it easy to find information without getting frustrated? This is a big issue when you use the Web in the classroom. You should always keep in mind that you won't always be able to connect to a Web site when you want to. Computer servers crash, and sometimes Web content is deleted or changed. When you find something on the Web that you want to use in class, it is often advisable to copy the page onto your own computer or a floppy disk, so you know you'll have it when you need it. If you plan to use a live Web connection in class, you should make sure that the site is easily available. And just in case, you should always have a backup plan in case there is a problem with your Internet server or the destination Web server.

Web design is also important. If you plan to introduce a Web site to your students and you expect them to use it in their learning, it is important that the site is interesting and interactive enough to be engaging. There are many fine Web sites designed to entice students to learn more about science, mathematics, and computer science.

If you are giving your students unsupervised access to the Internet, you probably should consider installing filtering software that can prevent students from visiting undesirable Web sites. Most school libraries have some sort of screen designed to prevent students from accessing pornography or hate-speech Web sites. Each institution has its own policy on what to filter or sensor. Screening software filters out any Web site that contains forbidden words or phrases. Some programs allow more sophisticated filtering conditions. And you want to make sure that you are not inadvertently blocking students from useful Web sites. By barring access to sites containing the word "sex" or references to anatomical parts, for example, students trying to do research on cancer or sex education could be hampered.

I have listed a number of Web sites of particular interest to K–12 teachers. First is a sampling of professional resources that are designed to help teachers do their jobs. There are also Web sites that are excellent examples of what you can do to bring the power of the Internet into your classroom. I have also compiled a list of some of the best Web sites to use in teaching a wide variety of disciplines, from history to physical education.

1) SCIENCE

Today, there are hundreds of Web sites dedicated to science education. Many are dedicated to K–12 education and funded by government agencies such as the U.S. Department of Education.

◆ *The example here shows how the fourth-grade science class at Hosmer School in Watertown, Massachusetts, is using the Web to show different types of volcanoes. The materials were created by students who are sharing their experiences with other students.*

FIGURE 5-1

◆ *The Science Learning Network is a project sponsored by the National Science Foundation and Unysis Corp. to create an online science learning community for teachers, students, and teaching institutions including museums and foreign schools. [www.sln.org]*

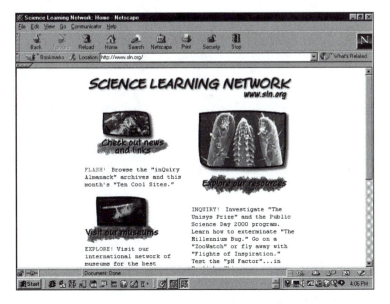

FIGURE 5-2

◆ *The Agricultural Research Service of the U.S. Department of Agriculture created a Web site for K–7 science classes. It provides some interactive features that can entice students to learn more about the subject. [http://www.ars.usda.gov/is/kids/]*

◆ *This example shows what applications chicken feathers have.*

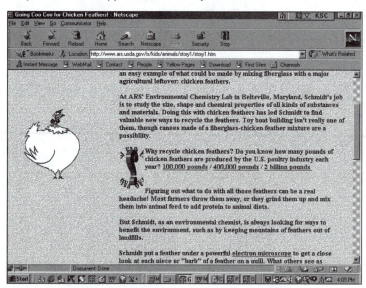

Another excellent Web site for science education is the one maintained by the British Broadcasting Corporation. The BBC has served the world-wide learning community since its inception with its radio programs. Now it is continuing its commitment to public education on the Web. This is a good site to use to investigate the nature and qualities of light. It provides a number of related ideas and examples. To visit the Web site, you need the following Web address: *http://www.bbc.co.uk/sia/.*

◆ This is a good site to use to investigate what light is. It provides a number of related ideas and examples.

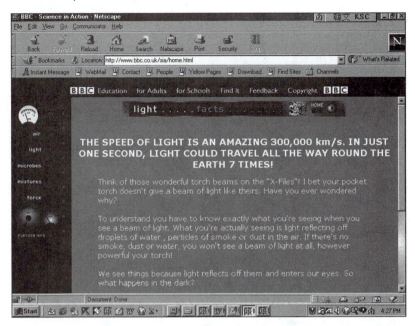

FIGURE 5-3

◆ Here is an interactive NASA site that deals with the space agency's research program investigating very-low-frequency radio signals in the earth's magnetosphere. High-school students who participate in this project assisted in setting up equipment and collecting data. [http://image.gsfc.nasa.gov/poetry/inspire/]

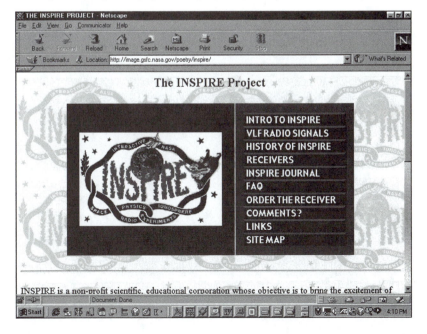

◆ *This example displays one of the spectrograms produced as part of the study.*

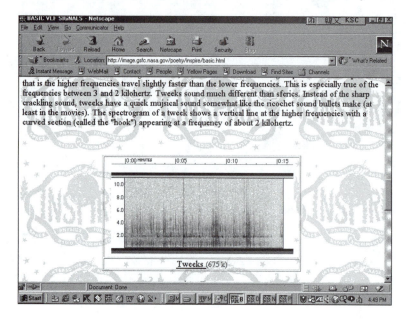

◆ *The National Museum of Natural History has a number of educational exhibits for students and teachers. This page is part of a special exhibition titled "In Search of Giant Squid."*

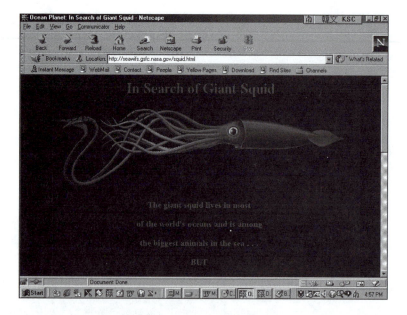

FIGURE 5-4

◆ *The Center for Educational Resources (CERES) Project is funded by NASA to develop an extensive library of online and interactive K–12 science-education materials for use in teaching astronomy. [http://btc.montana.edu/ceres/]*

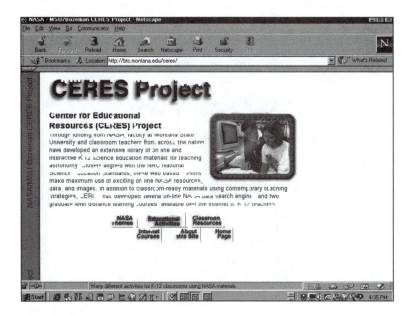

◆ *This example shows an Internet course in astronomy for 9–12 teachers.*

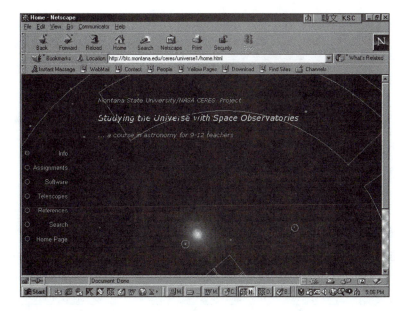

FIGURE 5-5

◆ *New York University's Science Teachers Enhancement Model is designed to foster an increase in the performance, participation and retention of students in K–12 science and mathematics to a level compliant with the New York State Education Department's student-performance standards. [http://www.nyu.edu/projects/mstep/menu.html]*

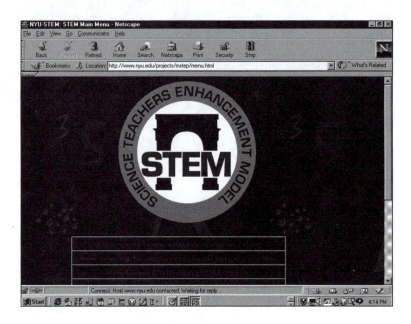

◆ *This example shows a middle-school lesson plan on "Aquatic Life in the Ocean."*

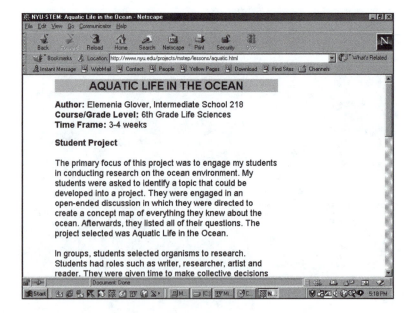

FIGURE 5-6

◆ *This Web site is provided by Los Alamos National Laboratory. It has a great interest in mathematics education and provides K–12 mathematics teachers with lots of useful teaching materials. [www.c3.lanl.gov/mega-math]*

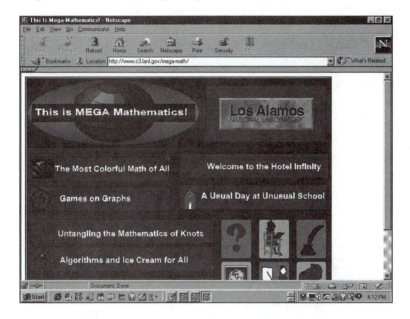

2) MATHEMATICS

World Wide Web has also opened exciting opportunities for mathematics teachers and students. In the pre-Web era, mathematics was a difficult subject to present online, since the Internet could not easily display equations, formulas, and images. The Web liberated mathematics education by allowing students to visualize mathematics. Studies have shown that this visualization is very important. The Web can also help students to engage in problem solving with interesting mathematics games.

◆ *This example shows mathematics activities related to graphic theory.*

FIGURE 5-7

◆ *The Math Forum is sponsored by the National Science Foundation and Swarthmore College. Its goal is to build an online community of teachers, students, researchers, parents, educators, and citizens at all levels who have an interest in math and math education.*

"Ask Dr. Math" is a project that helps students learn mathematics. Students can ask questions on the Web site and receive answers from experts.

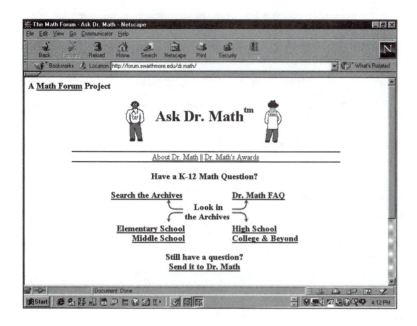

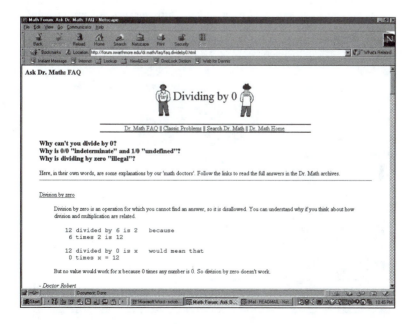

FIGURE 5-8

◆ *The National Council of Teachers of Mathematics (NCTM) is the largest nonprofit professional association of mathematics educators in the world. It has been dedicated to improving the teaching and learning of mathematics from kindergarten through college. It plays a crucial role in setting the curriculum standards.* [www.nctm.org]

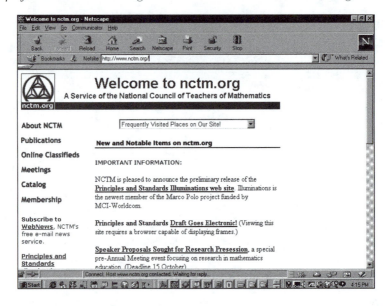

FIGURE 5-9

◆ *The Guide to Math and Science Reform received funding from the Annenberg Foundation and the Corporation for Public Broadcasting to educate and support families, teachers, teacher educators, administrators, policymakers, and others working to change the way math and science are taught.* [http://www.learner.org/theguide/]

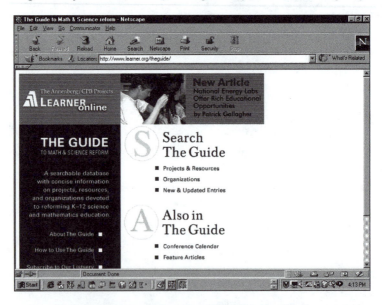

3) SOCIAL STUDIES

There are a number of social studies Web sites for teachers, parents, and students. Some are created by educational institutions, while others are created by companies who promote so-called edutainment products.

FIGURE 5-10

◆ *This is a good example of a Web site that is widely used in history courses. There are some good educational products that can be very helpful, but some of them focus more on entertainment than actual teaching and understanding of history. It is important for teachers and parents to investigate the products carefully before they recommend them to students.   http://oregon-trail.com*

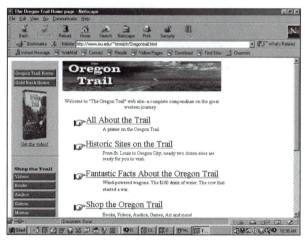

FIGURE 5-11

◆ *The End of the Oregon Trail Web site offers a number of useful teaching materials including some maps. Many Web sites offer similar information for teachers and students. These Web sites are very popular with history teachers.*
[http://endoftheoregontrail.org/maplibrary/oregontrail.html]

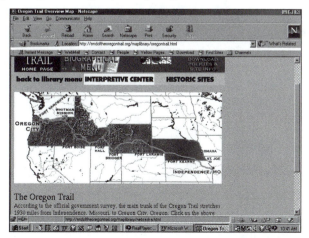

FIGURE 5-12

◆ *The Michael C. Carlos Museum at Emory University offers special exhibitions, lectures, films, and workshops including this online exhibition.*
[http://www.emory.edu/CARLOS/ODYSSEY/]

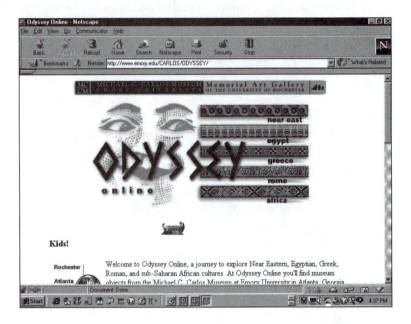

◆ *This shows the way of life in ancient Egypt.*

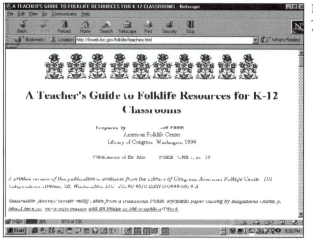

FIGURE 5-13

◆ *A Teacher's Guide to Folklife Resources for K–12 Classrooms is part of the Library of Congress Web site. [http://lcweb.loc.gov/folklife/teachers.html]*

4) ENGLISH, LITERATURE, AND WRITING-RELATED WEB SITES

There are many language arts-related Web sites. For style issues, you can check out the sites of the American Psychological Association—*http://www.apa.org/*; the Modern Language Association—*http://www.mla.org/* and the Library of Congress—*http://www.loc.gov/*. Another excellent site is produced by the Center for the Liberal Arts at the University of Virginia. *http://www.virginia.edu/~libarts/english.htm*

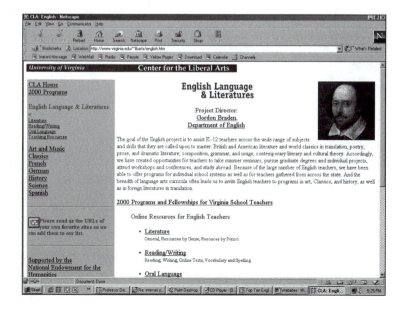

◆ *The Internet Classics Archive at MIT is an excellent source on the classics.*
http://classics.mit.edu/

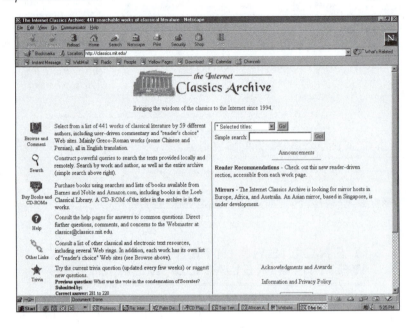

◆ *A great language-arts site focusing on African-American perspectives is*
http://www.thegateway.org/index2/languageartsliterature.html#9–12

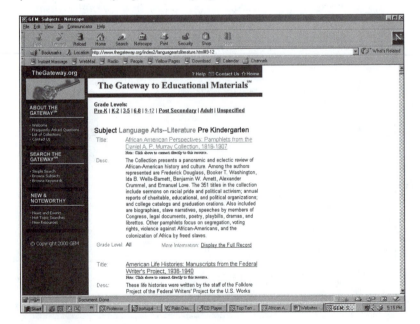

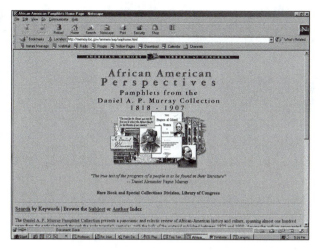

◆ *A site giving access to part of the Library of Congress's collection of African-American literature is at http://memory.loc.gov/ ammem/aap/aaphome. html*

You can find a very infomative site about author Langston Hughes at http://falcon.jmu.edu/!ramseyil/hughes.htm#D.

5) FOREIGN LANGUAGES

There are hundreds of foreign-language-related Web sites. The best are created by university language departments and professional organizations. Also, you can utilize foreign newspapers, such as the French-language *Le Monde [http://www.lemonde.fr/]* for foreign-language reading lessons.

FIGURE 5-14

◆ *The Tennessee Foreign Language Teaching Association at the University of Tennessee at Martin offers a mirror site of TFLTA. [http://www.utm.edu/departments/french/tflta.html]*

FIGURE 5-15

◆ *This foreign-language resources Web page provides a nice collection of foreign-language references. [http://www.itp.berkeley.edu/~thorne/HumanResources.html]*

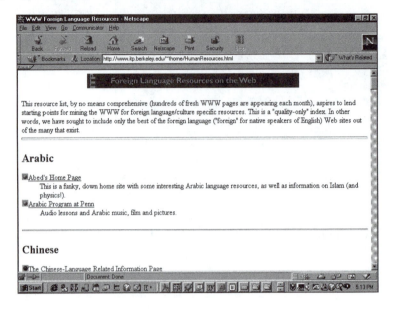

FIGURE 5-16

◆ *The National K–12 Foreign Language Resource Center at Iowa State University offers both summer institutes and workshops to prepare foreign-language educators with effective teaching strategies, new technologies, and performance assessment.*

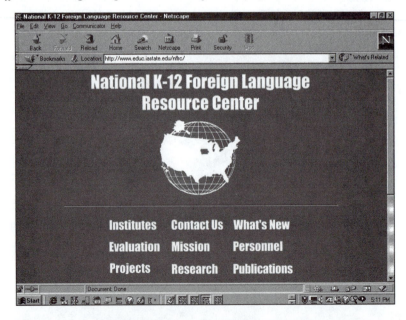

6) PHYSICAL EDUCATION AND HEALTH

Looking on the Web for sites related to physical education can be a real time waster, since searches tend to turn up a lot of unwanted sites. But there are some nice Web sites on the subject, especially those related to professional development.

FIGURE 5-17

◆ *The American Alliance for Health, Physical Education, Recreation and Dance is the largest organization of professionals supporting and assisting those involved in physical education, leisure, fitness, dance, health promotion, and education and all specialties related to achieving a healthy lifestyle. [http://www.aahperd.org]*

FIGURE 5-18

◆ *This Web site for physical education teachers, students, interested parents, and adults provides the latest information about contemporary developmentally appropriate physical education programs for children and youth. http://www.pecentral.org*

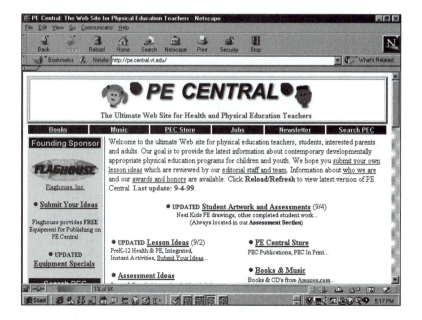

◆ *This Web site offers a number of useful lesson plans for teachers. This example shows a lesson on the "Human Body."*

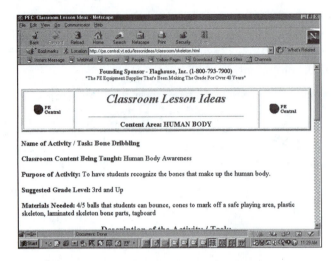

7) ART AND MUSIC

The World Wide Web has opened a new door for the public onto museums, art galleries, and music archives, allowing students access to collections of masterworks around the world.

FIGURE 5-19

◆ *This Guggenheim Museum Web site offers useful information about exhibitions that helps people understand paintings and artists. This activity is limited in the museum since there are too many paintings and too little time.*
http://www.pecentral.org/lessonideas/classroom/skeleton.html

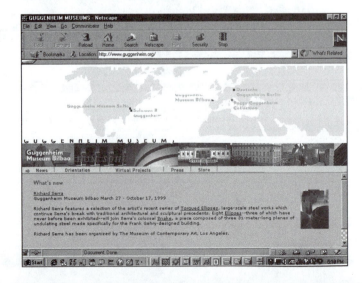

◆ *This provides information about a Clemente exhibition. Teachers and parents can decide if this is appropriate for younger students.*

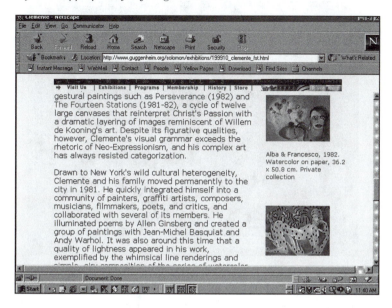

FIGURE 5-20

◆ *The Museum of Modern Art provides comprehensive materials for education as well as some exhibitions. [http://www.moma.org/]*

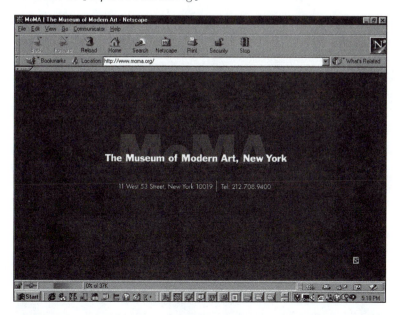

◆ *This shows a Van Gogh painting and provides background information with audio.*

The Metropolitan Museum of Art also has an extensive Web site that offers a tour of its many and varied art collections. Visit their Web site at *http://www.metmuseum.org.*

The Louvre Museum speaks for itself when it comes to art collections. It offers a number of programs in three major languages, an important plus for the non-English speaking K-12 education population. The Web site provides a virtual tour of the museum, which can be very useful for art teachers. To visit the Web site, you need the following Web address: *http://www.louvre.fr/.*

8) VOCATIONAL EDUCATION

FIGURE 5-21

◆ *Recently, vocational education has received much more attention, since continuing education is required for all workers. This Department of Education Web site provides comprehensive references for vocational education.* *[http://www.stw.ed.gov/]*

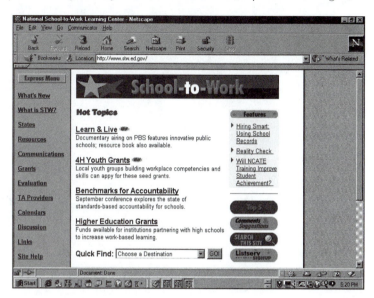

Part B

Internet-Based Curriculum Design

Building a Web Site

THE BASICS

Before doing anything else, it is a good idea to learn a few basic applications, such as a paint program and a simple Web-page editing program. These are usually included in your computer's operating system.

Next, you need to start thinking about the general layout—what you want your Web site to look like. It is often a good idea to look at other Web sites and even magazine spreads and other designs as you weigh your options. Then, sketch your proposed layout on a piece of paper and play with different ideas.

Always keep in mind the teaching goals of your Web site and the age of your audience. This should guide the organization and design. And remember: Most of the time, simpler is better. To get an even clearer idea of what will be effective with your students, you can get them involved in the design process, making the creation of the Web site a class project.

Once you've come up with the basic outline for what you want to include in your Web site, and how you want it to look, it is time to collect all of the elements—graphics, texts, video and audio clips, etc.—that you need. Most of them can probably be found on the Internet. When you find an image you want on the Internet, you press the right mouse button on the image and then select the "save image as" option from the shortcut menu you see. Then, you save the image on your local drive. You can collect animations, audio, and video files in the similar way. You can also buy small images known as clipart from software stores. One CD ROM disk can contain thousands of images and cost less than $20.

One thing you should be aware of is the size of the files you collect. Audio and video files can be huge and, if you are not careful, you can rapidly use up the space allotted for your Web page by your Internet Service Provider. Many ISPs limit Web-page storage space to 5 megabytes.

Some samples of clipart can be founded at http://normsgraphics.hypermart.net/images/Arrows/thumbs/arrow1.htm.

It can be fun and rewarding to get your students involved in the creation of their online classroom. Allowing students to contribute ideas and images and to participate in the design of the Web page will increase their sense of ownership of the project. And it will teach them a lot about the workings of the Internet and the World Wide Web.

When you have collected all the elements for your design, you must choose a program to help you assemble them all into a coherent whole. There are two basic ways to do this. One is by using off-the-shelf Web editor software. The other is by using HyperText Markup Language, or HTML. There are pros and cons to these two options.

Off-the-Shelf Web-Editor Software

Off-the-shelf Web-editor software can be purchased on the Internet or at your neighborhood software store, usually for less than $100. Most of these programs are developed so that anyone can publish a Web page without learning any HTML. These programs allow you to construct a Web page using the click-and-drag method. For the most part, you can just click on images and other elements that you want to include in your Web page and use the mouse to drag them into position. You can type in text content as if you were typing in a regular word-processing program. You can also add animations and text that scroll by as on a movie marquee.

FrontPage ($149) and HotDog Professional ($130) are well-known Web authoring programs. There are many others, and in terms of user-friendliness, features, and price, they are more or less the same. One important thing to keep in mind when using a Web editor, is that some of the special features don't work with all Web browsers. For example, if you use a Web editor to create scrolling text, it will produce a nice effect when your Web page is viewed using Internet Explorer. But if the page is viewed using the Netscape browser, it may be invisible.

FIGURE 6-1

◆ *FrontPage.*

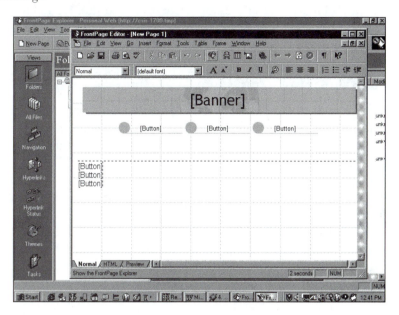

FIGURE 6-2

◆ *HotDog Professional.*

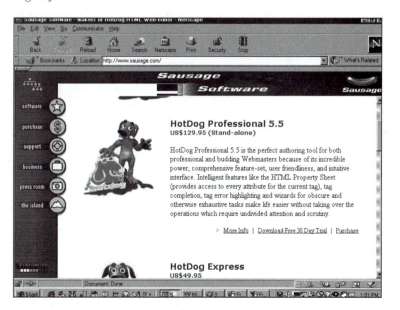

Using a Web editor is certainly the easiest way to start. But sometimes it can make things more complicated later, since you will need the Web editor software to make any subsequent changes to the site. It can also make it harder to fix any glitches that arise, since you will not be able to see the underlying computer code.

Customizing Your Own Web Page with HTML

If you don't want to depend on a Web-editor program, you can learn how to create a Web page from scratch using Hypertext Markup Language, or HTML, a set of commands that tells a computer how to run a Web page. Unlike other computer languages, such as C++ and Java, HTML is simple enough that you can learn the basics in a single day. There are plenty of books that can teach you the key HTML tags used in Web-page design.

To see how easy it can be to use HTML, let's create a simple Web page. You will need two programs, both of which should already be installed on your PC. The first is a simple editor program, such as Notepad, or any other simplified word-processing program. The second is your Web browser, which will allow you to test your work.

1. Create a workspace on your computer by creating a directory to store your Web pages. In Windows 95 or 98, first, open "My computer" and select the C: drive. Then you can create a folder by choosing "New folder" from the File menu. It is important that you know the basics of your operating system, whether it is a Macintosh System or Windows Operating System. These operating systems work more or less the same. Note: Wordpad is normally used for creating a larger-size document.

FIGURE 6-3

♦ *A side-by-side display of a Web page and the corresponding HTML code.*

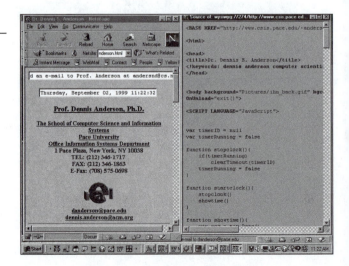

FIGURE 6-4

◆ *Working environment.*

2. Open the Notepad or a simple editor program, such as the one included with your operating system. A simple editor is a simplified
word-processing program, without all the fancy format features
you find in something like MS Word.

FIGURE 6-5

◆ *Simple text editors.*

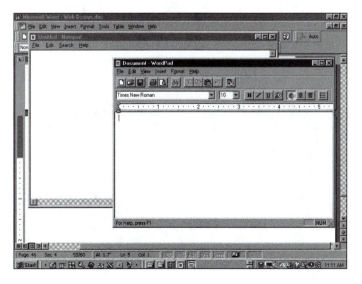

3. Open your Web browser. You can use either Netscape or Internet Explorer. Both programs can be obtained free of charge. You do not have to be online to create a Web page, as long as you have already assembled all of the materials you want to use. You will only need to be online when you are ready to upload (copy) your files to your Web server, so that other people can access your Web site.

4. Arrange these programs so that they overlap each other. That way you can easily switch back and forth if necessary. Using the Web browser allows you to test your HTML codes as you create your Web page.

FIGURE 6-6

◆ *Microsoft Internet Explorer.*

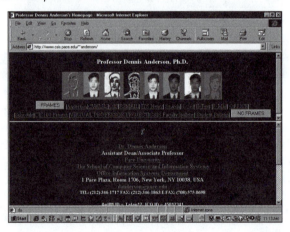

FIGURE 6-7

◆ *Netscape Navigator.*

FIGURE 6-8

◆ *Notepad and Netscape.*

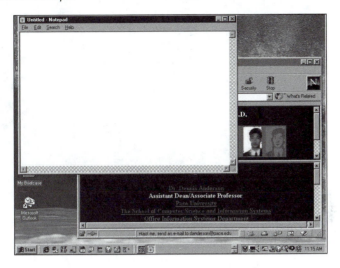

5. As a test, type the word "Hello" in Notepad.
6. Choose "Save As" from the File Menu, then select the folder you created from the "Look In" dialog box.

FIGURE 6-9

◆ *Saving a plain document.*

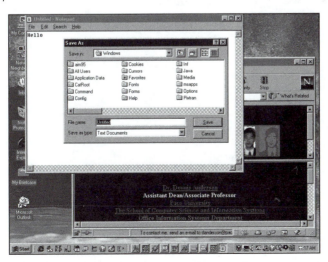

7. Select as the file type "text," then name the file myfirstpage.html. Make sure the file extension is html or htm.

FIGURE 6-10

◆ *Executing of Web page.*

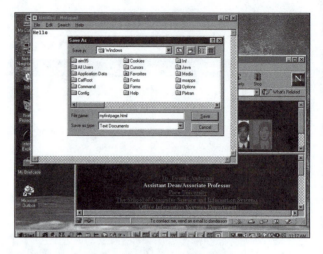

8. Now switch to Netscape for this exercise. Choose "Open" from the File menu. Select "Choose File" and then select the file you just saved in Notepad.

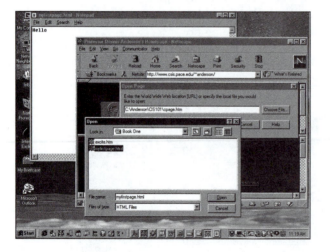

FIGURE 6-11

◆ *Opening a Web page.*

9. When you click on "Open," the computer will open your file in Netscape. From this exercise, you will see that even though we did not use any HTML tags, the plain text file comes out as a Web page. Then why learn HTML? The answer is to use special effects to create the much more sophisticated type of Web site that you see on the Internet. HTML will allow you to use different font sizes and styles, colors and images. But this exercise captures the basics that you need to know in order to create a simple Web page.

FIGURE 6-12

◆ *Executing of Web page.*

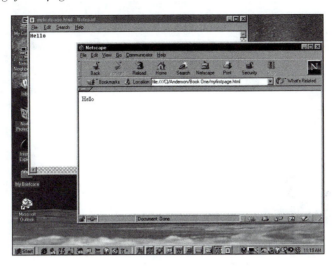

10. Now switch back to the Notepad and type "My name is Dennis" on the next line. Choose "Save" from the File menu, then click on "save as text." (You don't have to choose "Save As," since you are keeping the same file name.) Go back to Netscape and click on the "Reload" button to refresh the browser. Your two sentences will appear on the same line, instead of two.

FIGURE 6-13

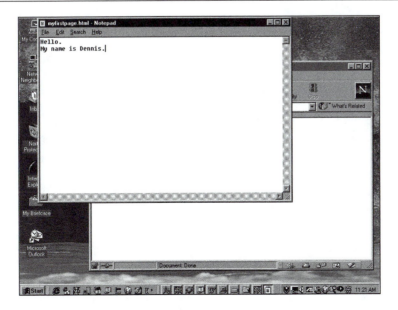

FIGURE 6-14

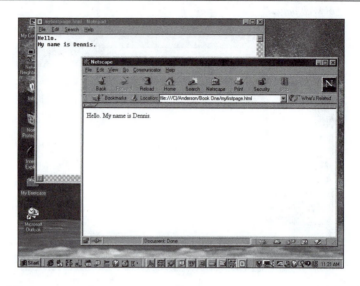

11. This is a good time to introduce you to a very useful tool. Most Web browsers have a built-in editor that can create HTML files for you. In Netscape Composer, the Netscape version of a Web editor, you choose "Edit Page" from the File menu. If you are creating a new Web page, you should choose "New" from the File menu. In the Web-editor screen, bring "My name is Dennis" to the line below "Hello," and then click on Save. Now click on Preview to see what happens. This time, the text will appear on two lines.

FIGURE 6-15

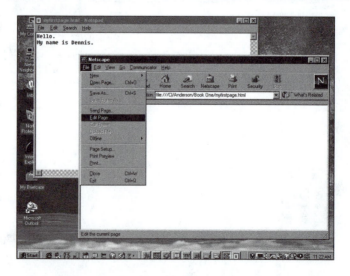

FIGURE 6-16

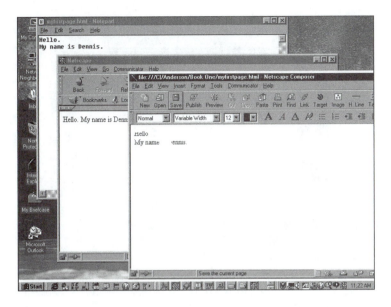

FIGURE 6-17

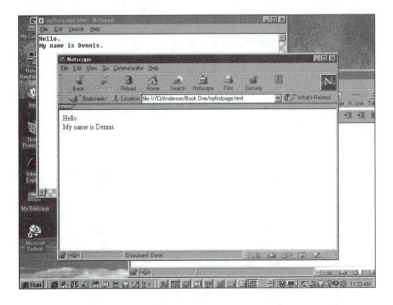

12. Switch back to Notepad and then close the current file without saving, since we changed the content of the file "myfirstpage.html" using Netscape Composer and you don't want to undo your changes. Now open "myfirstpage.html" again.

FIGURE 6-18

13. You will see now that the file has been changed dramatically with all
kinds of things you did not type in. These are the formatting codes
that were added when you saved the file in Composer. Composer con-
verted the file into an HTML file. These strange codes are known as
HTML tags. From these tags, you can see that a typical Web page is
divided into two sections, head and body. Tags contained within less-
than signs (also called open anchors) and greater-than signs (also
called close anchors) are invisible to the people who view the Web
page. Every set of tags has a beginning tag and an ending tag, such as
<html> and </html>. The ending tag has a slash before the tag name.

FIGURE 6-19

14. Now let's create a new Web page using HTML.
15. Switch to Notepad and choose New.
16. Type in a brief description of your Web page. This comment is for you or other people in case you want to edit the page. Comments are declared by using the open anchor followed by the "!" symbol. For example, <!doctype html public "-//w3c//dtd html 4.0 transitional//en">. This comment explains what kind of file it is and what version of English HTML was used.

FIGURE 6-20

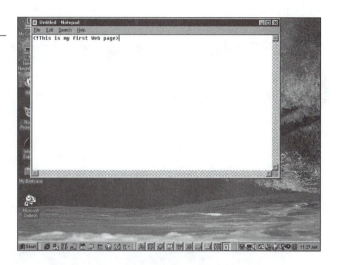

17. Type in <html> to indicate the beginning of your Web page then type in </html> to mark the ending. All other HTML tags will go in between these two tags.

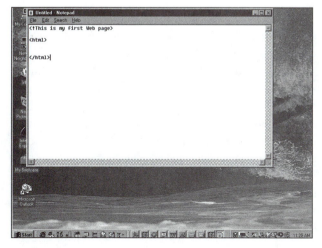

FIGURE 6-21

18. Type <head> and </head> for the heading, which usually includes the name of the author and the title of the Web page. This is the section where you can give a short description of the Web page. Inside the <head> tags, use the tags <title> and </title> to bracket the name of the Web page. For example, <title>My Main Web Page</title> will display the title of your Web page as "My Main Web Page."

FIGURE 6-22

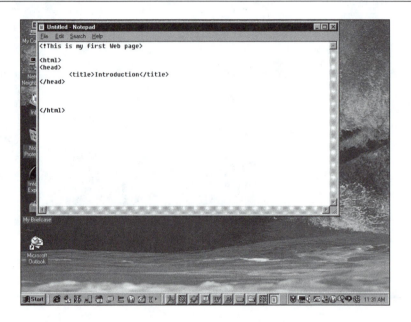

19. Type <body> to indicate the beginning of the main part of the Web page. The tag </body> will be used at the end of this section. This is where you specify how you want your Web page to actually look. With a few simple codes, you can choose a background image and color, as well as colors for text and hyperlinks. For example, <body background=sun.gif" bgcolor=#00FFFF" text=black link=red vlink=blue> will display a background image of the sky, black text color, and red hyperlinks that change to blue once they have been visited. If there is no such file as sun.gif, the background will be aqua. #00FFFF is a hexadecimal number that represents the color aqua. If you know the exact name of a color, there is no need to look up the hexadecimal number. This color table can be easily found on the Internet.

FIGURE 6-23

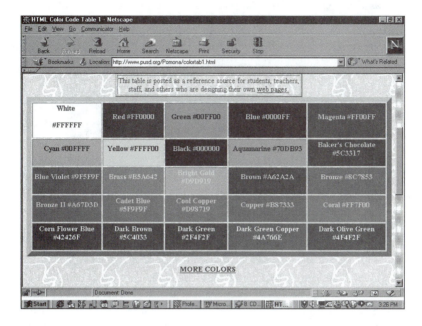

Now save your file as "mainpage.html." It should look like the following:

FIGURE 6-24

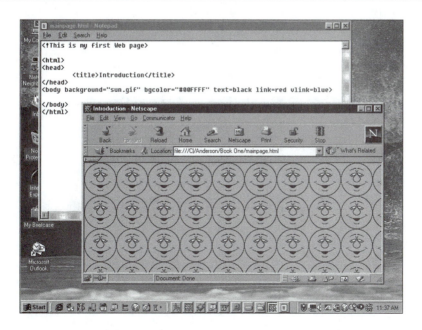

20. Type in the word "Hello" between body tags, then save the file again. Switch to Netscape and open the file to view your Web page.

FIGURE 6-25

21. Switch back to the Notepad and type <h1> and </h1> around the word "Hello." Save the change and reload the file in Netscape. <h1> indicates the size of the heading text. There are six different sizes indicated by the numbers 1 through 6. 1 is the largest. You can align the heading text by adding the align command. For example, <h1 align=center> will center the text that is enclosed between the "h" tags. Using a new set of "h" tags will automatically begin a new line of text.

FIGURE 6-26

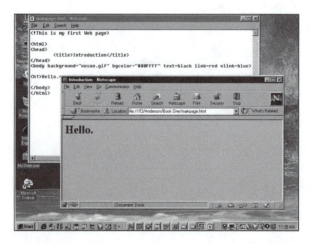

22. Now, type "My name is Dennis. I am a teacher." in the Notepad. Type in <br> after the first sentence. This tag will break these two sentences into two lines.

FIGURE 6-27

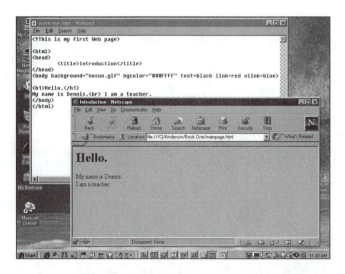

23. Exepriment by putting the tags <b>, <center>, <I>, <u>, and <blink> around "I am a teacher." Can you tell which tag did what? Pay attention to the closing sequences for the tags.

FIGURE 6-28

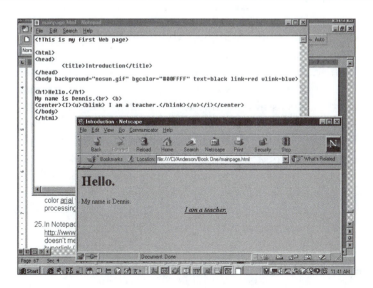

24. You can use the <font> tag to select the type face and size of text. For example, <font color=blue face=arial size=10>My office hours are 2-4 on Friday.</font> This will display the text in 10-point, arial-style font colored blue.

FIGURE 6-29

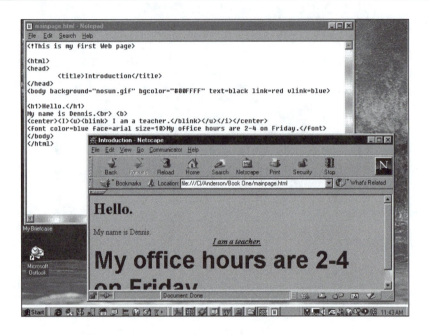

A) HYPERLINKS

25. In the Notepad, type in "My main Web page is located at *http://www.csis.pace.edu/~anderson.*" Just because you have a Web address it doesn't mean it will automatically link to that Web site. In order to make this a hyperlink—a virtual connection to another electronic document—you have to use the <A> tag. For instance, you can type "My main Web page is located at <a href=*http://www.csis.pace.edu/~anderson*">http://www.csis.pace.edu/~anderson</a>. In a similar way, you can give visitors to your Web site the chance to send e-mail to a specific address using a hyperlink. For example, you can type "My e-mail address is <a href=mailto:*danderson@pace.edu.*">danderson@pace.edu.</a>. The only difference is that "mailto" is used to open an e-mail program. Clicking on *danderson@pace.edu* will now open an e-mail program with *danderson@pace.edu* as the destination address. A <p> tag is used to insert a new paragraph.

FIGURE 6-30

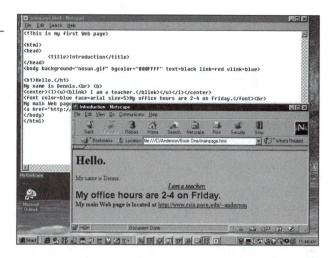

26. To insert an image into your Web page, you first have to prepare the image that you want to use.

B) DOWNLOADING IMAGES AND TEXTS

You can download an image (clipart or picture) from the Internet by putting your cursor over the image you want to download and clicking on the right button of your mouse. When you click you will get a menu of options. Select "Save image as." This will give you the file name of the image you selected. If you want to change the name, you can do so at this point. If not, you can select the location where you want to save the image file. It may be a good idea to put all image files into one directory.

Texts can be easily copied with the conventional copy-and-paste method. You can also save it by choosing "Save As" in Netscape. Then you can reuse the text you have saved later, when you are offline.

Warning: Although many images are in the public domain and free to copy without any permission, some are not. You should check carefully if there are any restrictions on the use of the images and text you select.

Downloading images from the Internet is inexpensive and easy. But if you are willing to spend the time to learn how to use a few painting and image-manipulation software programs such as Photo Shop and Paint Shop Pro, you can create high-quality images of your own.

Although there are many different file format types for images you find on the Internet, two are most common. The first is jpeg (pronounced Jay-peg), which stands for joint photographic experts group. The second is gif, (pronounced Gif), which is short for graphical interchange format. A gif file is conventionally used for smaller images. A jpeg file is used for large, high-quality images. Most image viewers can process these two types.

FIGURE 6-31

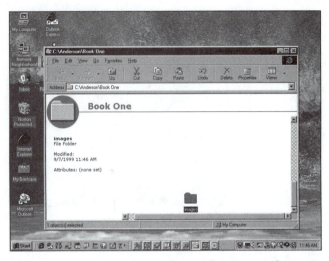

27. Type <img src="images/sun.gif"> in the Notepad.

FIGURE 6-32

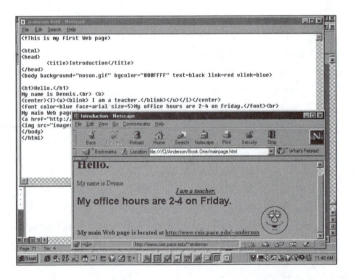

28. Now you can make this image into a hyperlink to a new page by typing <a href="nextpage.html"> around the img tag. For example, <a href="nextpage.html"><img src="images/sun.gif"></a>. This will make the sun image clickable. When you click on it, it will open the next page of your Web site. Since we do not yet have a second page, we have to create one.

FIGURE 6-33

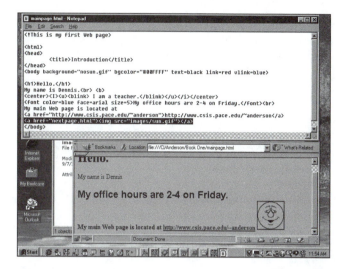

FIGURE 6-34

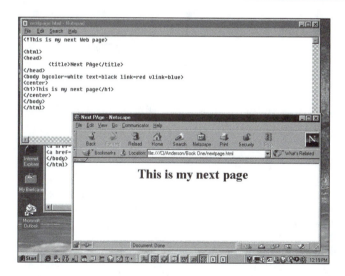

C) ELECTRONIC TABLES AND FORMS

In order to create a table, you need to get familiar with several new table-related tags and commands. These will allow you to specify a border, number of columns, their width, and the background color of the table. The <td> tag is used to enclose the text that will appear in an individual cell of the table, and the <tr> tag is used to enclose all the table cells within a single row. For example, <table border cols=3 width="100%" bg-color="#00FFFF"> will create a three-column table with a border, three columns, and an aqua-colored background. The table section is closed with a </table> tag. The easiest way to create a table is using a composer or Web editor. This will reduce the typos and errors.

FIGURE 6-35

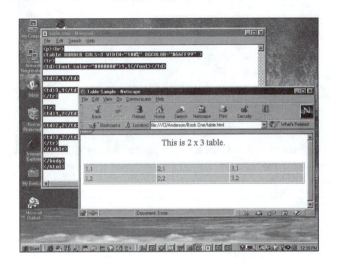

The source HTML codes for this Web page are:

<!doctype html public "-//w3c//dtd html 4.0 transitional//en">
<html>
<head>
    <meta http-equiv="Content-Type" content="text/html; charset=iso-8859-1">
    <meta name="Author" content="Dr. Dennis Anderson">
    <title>Table Sample</title>
</head>
<body>

<font color="#006600">
<font size=+2>This is 2 x 3 table.</font>
</font>

<p>
<table BORDER COLS=3 WIDTH="100%" BGCOLOR="#66FF99" >

```
<tr>
<td><font color="#000000">1,1</font></td>

<td>2,1</td>

<td>3,1</td>
</tr>

<tr>
<td>1,2</td>

<td>2,2</td>

<td>3,2</td>
</tr>
</table>
</body>
</html>
```

There are times you need a form to collect and process information. Often, they are used to collect survey data. With HTML, you can easily create an online survey form. First, you need to familiarize yourself with a few form-related tags. They are <form>, <input>, <option>, and <select>. The <form> tag indicates the beginning and end of a form. The <input> tag is

FIGURE 6-36

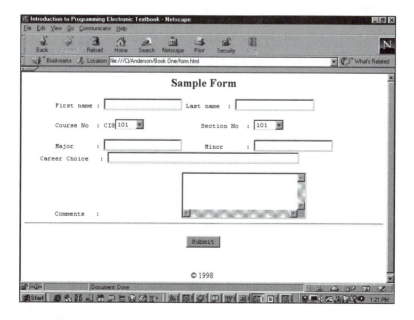

used to create various means for visitors to your site to respond to questions. You can use this tag to create check boxes, buttons, and spaces where visitors can type in an answer. You can also create a multiple-choice list using the <select> tag. Each item on the list is marked with an <option> tag.

The following Web page and HTML code will give you some idea of how these tags are used to create a list.

HTML Code

```
<html>
<head>
    <title>
    Introduction to Programming Electronic Textbook
    </title>
</head>
<body>
<center>
<h2>
Sample Form<dt>
</h2>
</center>
<p>
<FORM method="POST" action="http://www.csis.pace.edu/~ander-
    son/cgi-bin/store.pl">

<pre>
    First name : <input type="text" name="firstname"
onfocus="prompt('first name')"> Last name : <input type="text"
name="lastname">

        Course No : CIS<select name="class">
            <option value="101">101
            <option value="111">111
            <option value="201A">201A
            <option value="301">301
            <option value="600A">600A
            <option value="600B">600B
            <option value="700">700
            </select>    Section No : <select
name="section">
```

```
<option value="1">61138
<option value="2">90084
</select>
```

Major : <input type="text" name="major"
onfocus="prompt('major')"> Minor : <input type="text"
name="minor" onfocus="prompt('minor')")><dt> Career Choice :
   <input
type="text" name="career" size=50>

Comments :
<textarea name="comments" rows=4 cols=30>
</textarea>
<hr>

<input type="submit" value="Submit">
</form>

</pre>

© 1998

</body>
</html>

There are a few interesting things to note. The <hr> tag creates a horizontal line. You can create a copyright symbol by looking up an HTML special-character table on the Internet and copying it. The <pre> tag is used to preserve the format and spacing as it is in an HTML file.

A number of Web sites provide a special HTML character table that shows a standard character set. You can either use a numeric code or descriptive code to create a special character that is not normally included among the keys on your keyboard. For example, a pound sign can be created using the descriptions "&#163" or "&pound." You have to have the "&" sign in order to see the symbol.

Lists

If you have a number of items that you want to display as a list, you can use either <UL> or <OL> tags. The <UL> tag is used to list unordered items and the <OL> tag is used to list ordered items. Each item in the list must be enclosed in <LI> tags as shown in the following example.

FIGURE 6-37

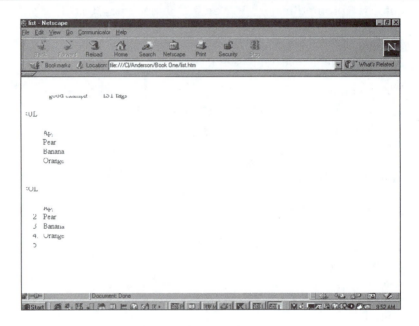

FIGURE 6-38

Adding Frames

You also can divide your screen into frames as in the following displays.

You can divide space horizontally or vertically or both, depending on how you want to arrange items on your screen. This technique can be used to display a variety of information on one screen rather than requiring a visitor to open many different screens. For instance, if I choose the "Search" option in the top frame, it will open the Search page in the bottom frame.

FIGURE 6-39

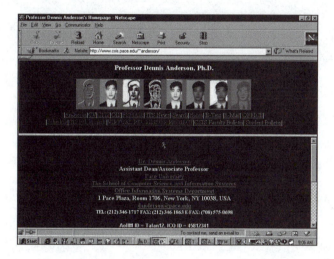

FIGURE 6-40

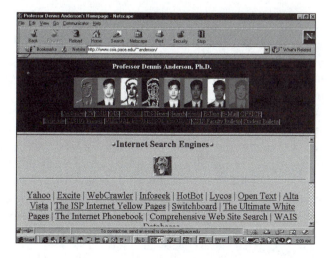

You can have as many frames as you want, but adding too many can make your page difficult to read and access. Two or three frames for a Web page are usually adequate. In order to create a Web page with two frames, you have to have three HTML files. Two are normal HTML files that you see on the screen. The other is an index file that tells how to organize the other two frames.

FIGURE 6-41

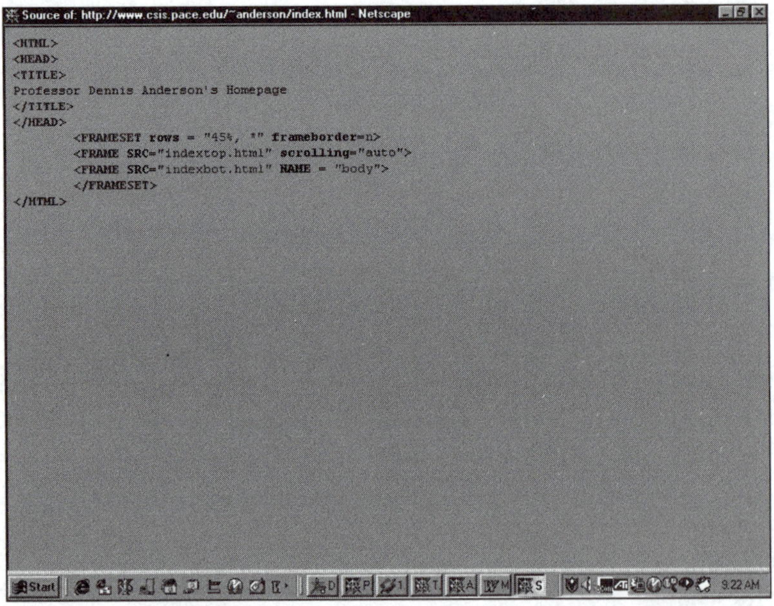

The index file is the one a Web browser looks for if no name is specified after the Web address domain. For example, if you type *http://www.csis.pace.edu/~anderson/* into a browser, the browser will look for an index file. This is what we normally mean by the main Web page.

As you see in the above HTML source code, dividing your screen into frames requires <frameset> and <frame> tags. The <frameset> tag dictates how many frames you want to have, how large they will be, and whether they will divide the screen horizontally or vertically. (An "*" can be used to refer to the remainder of the space not already taken up.) The <frame> tag is used to list the items you want to have in a given frame and tell how you want to organize them. If you have more than two frames in a screen, you can also create nested frame sets, with additional frames contained within the original frames.

D) TELNET AND FTP

Telnet and FTP (File Transfer Protocol) are important tools for teachers who want to design their own Web pages. In order to make the Web pages available at anytime, they must be stored on a special computer called a server. In order to access the server and modify the Web pages, you need a program to log in to the server from your PC. That's what telnet programs allow you to do. You can log in to your server from anywhere with telnet and check your e-mail and create Web pages.

FTP is a program that allows you to upload and download programs from your PC to the Internet server and vice versa. FTP programs and telnet programs can be easily downloaded from the Internet. These programs are fairly easy to use. Some FTP programs let the user edit Web contents remotely and then, with a click, update their files on the server.

Telnet programs also allow you to log on anonymously to many servers. For example, you can log in to a remote library catalogue. If you want to find a book in the New York University library, for example, you would type in bobcat.nyu.edu in a telnet program and then type in "anonymous" as a username and your e-mail address as a password. This tool gives you access that is very valuable for research.

FIGURE 6-42

◆ *Anonymous login to public systems.*

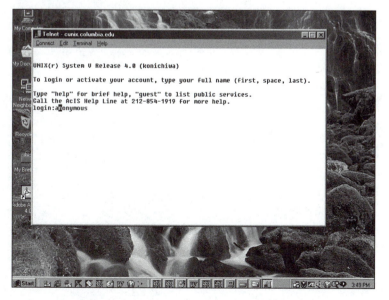

CHAPTER 7

Advanced Lessons

A) CREATING VIRTUAL CLASSROOMS

In order to create a virtual classroom that can be used as a supplement to your bricks-and-mortar classroom or as an after-school class, you should think about the following.

- You need to consider a mixture of different technologies on the Internet.
- You need to carefully evaluate these technologies.
- You should survey your students for their technological fluency and their access to computers outside of school.
- You should adopt only technologies that are appropriate for your students' use.
- You should think about how much time this project will require.
- What is most important to you as a teacher in terms of teaching the content?
- What is most important to your students in terms of learning the content?
- You should design your Web site to complement your lesson plans.

B) OTHER RECOMMENDATIONS

Think 3D

You should think in three dimensions when you design an interactive environment for cyber learning. It is easy for an instructor to create a long list of things on the Web page that forces students to scroll up and down to choose a hyperlink. Building a Web site that graphically mirrors an actual classroom is much more engaging. This is a time-consuming task, but it allows you to place at your students' fingertips essential tools for learning. It also allows you to filter out the tremendous distractions of the World Wide Web.

FIGURE 7-1

Maps, dictionaries, thesauruses, books, calculators, and other common classroom tools can be easily re-created in your new, virtual space. And you don't have to reinvent the wheel. While you want to make sure that the content of your cyber classroom is tailored to the needs of your students and your teaching goals, it is okay to mine the rich resources of the Internet. There are maps, dictionaries, thesauruses, language translators, books, calculators, and currency converters already out there in cyber space. And adding them to your cyber classroom will enrich your students' experience.

FIGURE 7-2

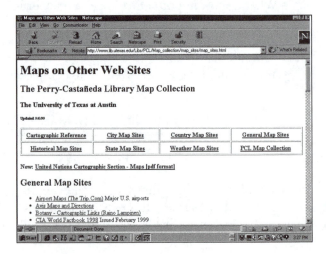

FIGURE 7-3

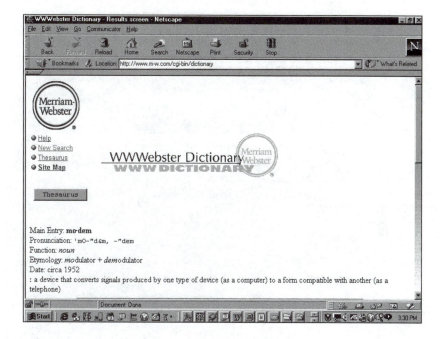

FIGURE 7-4

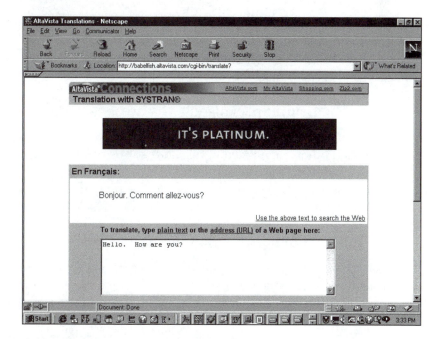

FIGURE 7-5

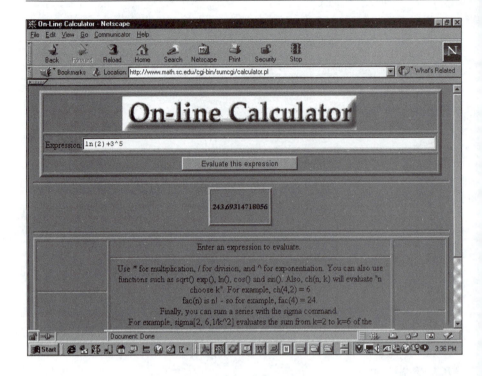

Cyber Slide Shows

You can pick a theme and present a sequence of Web slides to create a slide show that students can use independently as a tutorial. This would also make a good group project for your students.

Learn Specialized Software

To pull this off, you should learn specialized software such as Photo Shop, Sound editor, and others mentioned in this book so you can be more creative in your Web design. You can learn some of these programs in a day or two, though some require classroom training to use properly. There also are hundreds of books on these topics.

Online Homework Assignments and Tests

To really make the cyber classroom work, you need to get your students used to using it regularly. One way to do this is to communicate with your students through the Web site often. You can send e-mails and engage them in chat conferences. Assignments can be posted on the Web site. You can even have students submit homework and take tests and quizzes online.

Connecting to Video and Audio Materials

You also can connect digital video cameras and microphones to broadcast over your Web page, but this requires specialized hardware and software. It can also be quite expensive to feed a live video stream over the Internet, especially if you have a slow connection. To use a Web cam, you must purchase a digital video camera and Webcam program that will create sequential images for your Web audience. That way you can carry live broadcasts on your Web site.

You can also transmit power-point presentations or music, speeches, and other audio feeds over the Internet. But, as with video, they often require expensive technology. And if your viewers don't have the right equipment, they can't make use of these features anyway. When you design your Web page, you should keep in mind that many of your students won't have fancy computers at home.

If you want to view streaming video or listen to streaming audio in class, it is probably best done by logging onto a Web site that specializes in that. Using these Web sites provides a good opportunity to talk with older students about Internet ethics, especially the issues of voyeurism and a person's right to privacy.

FIGURE 7-6

◆ *Here, a Webcam shows the corner of Fifth Avenue on 45th Street in Manhattan. It can be programmed to feed the images live or change them once every few minutes.*

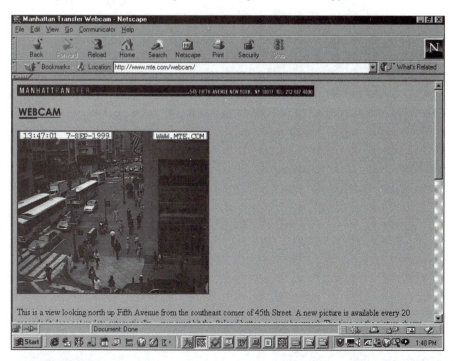

Here, a Webcam shows the corner of Fifth Avenue and 45th Street in New York City. It can be programmed to feed live images continuously, or to transmit a new snapshot every few minutes.

Creating Chat Rooms

You can create chat rooms online that allow your students to talk to teachers and each other. As we have already discussed, there is something called Internet Relay Chat, or IRC, which can be downloaded for free and allows you to chat with other IRC members by using the IRC number. You can also create your own chat room, if you want to control who can join in the chat. That way you can create a chat room open only to members of your class and their guests.

FIGURE 7-7

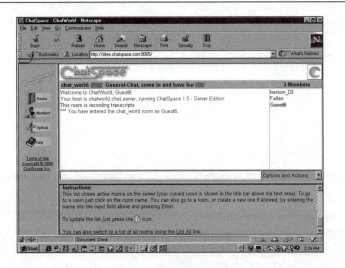

Creating School-Wide Networks

You can start a small cyber classroom for your class first. But this concept can be extended to encompass the entire school. Teachers' classroom Web sites can be linked together. And administrators can join in as well.

Web Pages to Communicate with Parents

Many parents today are too busy to come to PTA meetings or visit you and your classroom as often as they should. If you have a cyber classroom you can make it possible for parents to get information and even to participate in class activities from home. In this way, the cyber classroom can help build a larger school community including parents.

Student Grades, Attendance, and Other Records

You can make students' grades, attendance, and other records available to students' parents over the Internet. You can also provide a graph of how students are performing in your class relative to the other children.

Lesson Plans

You can also make your lesson plans available on your Web site so that students and parents can use them to prepare for the next day or catch up if a student is absent.

Student Clubs

You can also create a student section of the Web page, so that individual students can organize their activities and do things on their own. This will encourage students to explore their ideas and help them expand their horizons.

Education-Related Listservs

- **Academic Information Exchange**, send the message "sub ACADINFO your name" to listserv@listserv.iupui.edu
- **Quality of Academic Environment—NASULGC**, send the message "sub ACADQUAL your name" to listserv%sdsuvm.bitnet@listserv.net
- A list for use for **Distance Education** on Active Learning, send the message "sub ACTIVE-L your name" to listserv@admin.humberc.on.ca
- **Adult Education** Teaching Methods List, send the message "sub ADLTMETH-L your name" to listserv@tamuk.edu
- Adult Basic and Literacy **Education Professional Development**, send the message "sub AEPDCC your name" to listserv@tamvm1.tamu.edu
- American **Educational Research** Association List (AERA), send the message "sub AERA your name" to listserv@asuvm.inre.asu.edu
- **Educational Administration** Forum, send the message "sub AERA-A your name" to listserv@asuvm.inre.asu.edu
- **Educational History** and Historiography, send the message "sub AERA-F your name" to listserv@asuvm.inre.asu.edu
- **Social Context of Education**, send the message "sub AERA-G your name" to listserv@asuvm.inre.asu.edu
- **School Evaluation and Program Development**, send the message "sub AERA-H your name" to listserv@asuvm.inre.asu.edu
- Teaching and **Teacher Education**, send the message "sub AERA-K your name" to listserv@asuvm.inre.asu.edu

- **Educational Policy** and Politics, send the message "sub AERA-L your name" to listserv@asuvm.inre.asu.edu
- Educational Research Forum on **Minority Issues**, send the message "sub AERA-MI your name" to listserv@listserv.unb.ca
- Association for **Humanistic Education** and Development, send the message "sub AHEADNET your name" to listserv@vm.sc.edu
- AJCU Conference on **Teacher Education**, send the message "sub AJCUEDU your name" to listserv@listserv.georgetown.edu
- A forum to discuss **alternative approaches to learning**, send the message "sub ALTLEARN your name" to listserv@stjohns.edu
- **Computer applications in science and education**, send the message "sub APPL-L your name" to listserv@man.torun.pl
- Discussions about **Autism**, send the message "sub autism first-name last-name" to listserv@maelstrom.stjohns.edu
- Forum for Discussion of **Research on Bilingualism** and Bilingual Education, send the message "sub biling first-name last-name" to listserv@asu.edu
- Educational Resources on the **Internet**, send the message "sub C-EDRES your name" to listserv@listserv.unb.ca
- Coalition of Essential **Schools News**, send the message "sub CESNEWS your name" to listserv@brownvm.brown.edu
- Comparative and **Global Studies** in Education, send the message "sub CGSE-L your name" to listserv@listserv.acsu.buffalo.edu
- **Charter Schools** List, send the message "sub CHARTERSCHOOLS your name" to listserv@listserv.syr.edu
- **Chemistry Education** Discussion List, send the message "sub CHEMED-L your name" to listserv@uwf.cc.uwf.edu
- **Computer Networks** in Education, send the message "sub CNEDUC-L your name" to listserv@tamvm1.tamu.edu
- Colleges and High Schools **Co-Operative Learning** Group, send the message "sub COLRN-L your name" to listserv@admin.humberc.on.ca
- COMUEDUC—Dialogue Concerning **Public Community**, send the message "sub COMUEDUC your name" to listserv@vm.sc.edu
- CREAD Workshop on **Distance Education Quality Control**, send the message "sub CREAD-D your name" to listserv@yorku.ca
- Forum for Instructors of **Distance Education**, send the message "sub DE-L your name" to listserv@pdomain.uwindsor.ca
- DEOS-L-The **Distance Education Online Symposium**, send the message "sub DEOS-L your name" to listserv@psuvm.psu.edu

- **Distance Education Online Research**, send the message "sub DEOS-R your name" to listserv@cmuvm.csv.cmich.edu
- DEOSNEWS-The **Distance Education** Online Symposium, send the message "sub DEOSNEWS your name" to listserv@psuvm.psu.edu
- **Distance Education** Research Roundtable, send the message "sub DERR-L your name" to listserv@cmuvm.csv.cmich.edu
- Dialogues in **Methods of Education**, send the message "sub DIME-L your name" to listserv@postoffice.cso.uiuc.edu
- Educational activities at **Discovery Channel Online**, send the message "sub DISCOVERY-SCHOOL your name" to listserv@lists.discovery.com
- DISSMN8—**Disseminating Educational Theory and Practice**, sending the message "sub DISSMN8 your name" to listserv%ucbcmsa.bitnet@listserv.net
- **Early childhood education**/young children (0-8), send the message "sub ECENET-L your name" to listserv@postoffice.cso.uiuc.edu
- **Early Childhood Education** online mailing list, send the message "sub ECEOL-L your name" to listserv@maine.maine.edu
- **Educational Administration** Discussion List, send the message "sub EDAD-L your name" to listserv@wvnvm.wvnet.edu
- **U.S. Department of Education Information**, sending the message "subscribe EDINFO your name" to listproc@inet.ed.gov
- **Philosophy of Education**, open access, send the message "sub EDPHIL2-L your name" to listserv@postoffice.cso.uiuc.edu
- **Educational Reform** Discussion Group, send the message "sub EDREF-L your name" to listserv@admin.humberc.on.ca
- **Educational Resources** on the Internet—Database, send the message "sub EDRES-DB your name" to listserv@listserv.unb.ca
- EDTECH—**Educational Technology**, sending the message "sub EDTECH your name" to LISTSERV@H-NET.MSU.EDU
- **Educational Special Interest** List, send the message "sub EDUSIG-L your name" to listserv@ubvm.cc.buffalo.edu
- **Education and information technologies**, send the message "sub EDUTEL your name" to listserv@vm.its.rpi.edu
- **Educational Equity**, send the message "sub EQUITY-L your name" to listserv@american.edu
- **Educational Research** List (ASUACAD), send the message "sub ERL-L your name" to listserv@asuvm.inre.asu.edu
- **European academy of teachers** in general practice, send the message "sub EURACT your name" to listserv@cc1.kuleuven.ac.be
- **Geology and Earth Science** Education Discussion Forum, send the message "sub GEOED-L your name" to listserv@uwf.cc.uwf.edu

- **Global Studies** High School, send the message "sub GLBL-HS your name" to listserv@ocmvm.cnyric.org
- Discussion of **TI Graphing Calculators** in Education, send the message "sub GRAPH-TI your name" to listserv@peach.ease.lsoft.com
- Great Expectations **Teaching for K-12**, send the message "sub GREATEX your name" to listserv@uafsysb.uark.edu
- An H-Net List for **Teaching Social Studies** in Secondary Schools, send the message "sub H-HIGH-S your name" to listserv@msu.edu
- HERNTALK—**Houston Education** Resource Network (HERN) forum, send the message "sub HERNTALK your name" to listserv@listserv.rice.edu
- **High School Scholastic Journalism**, send the message "sub HSJOURN your name" to listserv@vm.cc.latech.edu
- HYPEREDU : **Hypertext in education**, send the message "sub HYPEREDU your name" to listserv%itocsivm.bitnet@listserv.net
- RI IEARN **Education and Youth Projects**, send the message "sub IEARNRI your name" to listserv@uriacc.uri.edu
- **Psychoanalysis and Education** send the message "sub IFPE your name" to listserv@listserv.kent.edu
- Institute for **Math and Science** Education, send the message "sub IMSE-L your name" to listserv@listserv.uic.edu
- International Society for **Education Through Art**, send the message "sub INSEA-L your name" to listserv@listserv.unb.ca
- International Development and **Global Education**, send the message "sub INTDEV-L your name" to listserv@uriacc.uri.edu
- **Technology in Education** Mailing List, send the message "sub JEI-L your name" to listserv%umdd.bitnet@listserv.net
- **Open Lib/Info Science Education** Forum, send the message "sub JESSE your name" to listserv@utkvm1.utk.edu
- ND **K-12 Geography** Educators, send the message "sub K-12GE-OGED your name" to listserv@listserv.nodak.edu
- K-12 Educators Interested in **Educational Administration**, send the message "sub K12ADMIN your name" to listserv@listserv.syr.edu
- **The K-12 Assessment** List, send the message "sub K12ASSESS-L your name" to listserv@lists.cua.edu
- A Forum for Education in Small or Rural Schools, send the message "sub K12SMALL your name" to listserv@uafsysb.uark.edu
- **K-12 Web Development** Mailing List, send the message "subscribe K12-WEBDEV your name" to list@mail.lr.k12.nj.us
- Kids—**PreSchool** discussion list, send the message "sub KIDS-PR your name" to listserv@vm3090.ege.edu.tr

- Discussion Group for **Course Education in Kindergarten**, send the message "sub KINDEDU your name" to listserv@listserv.kent.edu
- **Kentucky K-12 Arts and Humanities** Teachers Discussion List, send the message "sub KYARTS your name" to listserv@lsv.uky.edu
- **Kentucky K-12 Math Teachers** Discussion List, send the message "sub KYMATH your name" to listserv@lsv.uky.edu
- Teaching writing to individuals with **learning disabilities** and/or attention deficit disorder, send the message "subscribe LDCOMP" to listserv@home.ease.lsoft.com
- **Learning Disability** Discussion List, send the message "subscribe LD-LIST" to majordomo@curry.edu
- School **Library Media & Network Communications**, send the message "sub LM_NET your name" to listserv@listserv.syr.edu
- Provide support and information to **K-12 teachers**, send the message "sub LRN-ED your name" to listserv@listserv.syr.edu
- **Maryland K-12** Classroom Teachers, send the message "sub MDK-12 your name" to LISTSERV@UMDD.UMD.EDU
- **Mediation in Education**, send the message "sub MEDED-L your name" to listserv@postoffice.cso.uiuc.edu
- **Media in Education**, send the message "sub MEDIA-L your name" to listserv@bingvmb.cc.binghamton.edu
- **Middle level education**/early adolescence (10–14), send the message "sub MIDDLE-L your name" to listserv@postoffice.cso.uiuc.edu
- **Montessori Education** Discussion List, send the message "sub MONTESSORI-L your name" to listserv@listserv.aol.com
- **Multicultural Education** Discussion, send the message "sub MULTC-ED your name" to listserv%umdd.bitnet@listserv.net
- **Language and Education** in Multi-Lingual Settings, send the message "sub MULTI-L your name" to listserv@vm.biu.ac.il
- **Midwest Education Research** Association—H, send the message "sub MWERA-H your name" to listserv@vm1.cc.uakron.edu
- National Center for **Academic Integrity**, send the message "sub NCAI-L your name" to listserv%umdd.bitnet@listserv.net
- Reform discussion list for **Science Education**, send the message "sub NCPRSE-L your name" to listserv@ecuvm.cis.ecu.edu
- **National Council of Teachers of English** Discussion, go to http://www.ncte.org/lists/ncte-talk/ and filling in the form.
- Workshops For **Grades K-12:** New Designs For Learning, send the message "sub NETDESIG your name" to listserv@iubvm.ucs.indiana.edu

- Workshops For **Grades K-12:** Applications of the Internet, send the message "sub NETINTRO your name" to listserv@iubvm.ucs. indiana.edu
- Workshops For **Grades K-12:** Creating Internet Servers, send the message "sub NETSERV your name" tolistserv@iubvm.ucs.indiana.edu
- Workshops For **Grades K-12:** Internet Searching for Educators, send the message "sub NETSRCH your name" to listserv@iubvm.ucs.indiana.edu
- **Nursing Education,** send the message "sub NURSED-L your name" to listserv@psuvm.psu.edu
- Open forum for **Mathematics Education** Leadership in Ohio, send the message "sub OMELC your name" to listserv@listserv.kent.edu
- Teaching **High School Psychology**, send the message "sub PSYCH-NEWS your name" to listserv@listserv.uh.edu
- **School psychologists**—Assessment & intervention send the message "sub PSYCHOEDUCATIONAL_ASSESS your name" to listserv@listserv.arizona.edu
- **Mathematics, Science, and Technology Education** Group, send the message "sub QMSTE-L your name" to listserv@qucdn.queensu.ca
- **Continuing Medical Education** Discussion List, send the message "sub SMCDCME your name" to listserv@cms.cc.wayne.edu
- **Sociocultural Approaches to Mathematics** Education, send the message "sub SOCIOMATH-L your name" to listserv@listserv.acsu.buffalo.edu
- **Science/Math Education** Information, send the message "sub SP-SCIENCE-MATH-EDUCATION-LIST your name" to listserv@listserv.acsu.buffalo.edu
- **Special Education** Discussion List, send "sub SPECED-L your name" to listserv@uga.cc.uga.edu
- **History of American Education** study group, EDCI @ TAMU & UT, send the message "sub SWCLIO your name" to listserv@tamvm1.tamu.edu
- **Teaching Science in Elementary Schools,** send the message "sub T321-L your name" to listserv@mizzou1.missouri.edu
- **Talented and Gifted Education**, send the message "sub TAG-L your name" to listserv@listserv.nodak.edu
- News and Information for K-12 Teachers in **Rhode Island**, send the message "sub TEACH-RI your name" to listserv@uriacc.uri.edu
- TESL-L: **Teachers of English as a Second Language** List, send the message "sub TESL-L your name" to listserv@cunyvm.cuny.edu

- TESLIE-L: **Intensive English Program** (TESL-L sublist), send the message "sub TESIE-L your name" to listserv@cunyvm.cuny.edu, but you must first be subscribed to TESL-L.
- **Critical Thinking**, send the message "sub THINK-L your name" to listserv@umslvma.umsl.edu
- **Art Education** Issues, send the message "sub UAARTED your name" to listserv@listserv.arizona.edu
- **Berkeley Vocational Education** Discussion L, send the message "sub VOCNET your name" to listserv%ucbcmsa.bitnet@listserv.net
- **K-12 School** Network, send the message "sub VT-HSNET your name" to listserv@vtvm1.cc.vt.edu
- **Workplace** Education List, send the message "sub WORKPLAC your name" to listserv@maine.maine.edu
- Ruralnet Forum on **Computer Networking in Education**, send the message "sub WVRK12-L your name" to listserv@wvnvm.wvnet.edu

Education-Related Newsgroups

- K–12 newsgroups
  These newsgroups are specifically designed for students and educators from Kindergarten to Grade 12.
- Alt.education newsgroups
  These newsgroups are general Internet Usenet newsgroups.
- Misc.education newsgroups
  These newsgroups are another general Internet Usenet newsgroups.

Glossary

- Application: Software designed for a specific purpose.
- E-mail: Electronic mail.
- FTP (File Transfer Protocol): A program that allows files to be transferred electronically between your computer and others.
- Host computer: A computer connected to the Internet where Web pages are stored.
- HTML (Hyper Text Markup Language): Standard programming script language for Web pages.
- Internet Service Provider (ISP): A company that provides access to the Internet.
- Mainframe: A large computer system that is used to handle most computation-intensive tasks.
- Modem (Modulator-demodulator): Allows two computers to communicate by converting analog telephone signals to digital computer signals.
- Multimedia computer: A computer that allows the user to view video and listen to audio.
- OS (Operating Systems): The software that controls and manages the entire operation of a computer.
- Search engine: Web-based software that enables users to find information on the Web.
- Telnet: A program that allows a user to connect to a remote computer such as a mainframe.
- URL (Uniform Resource Locator): The address of a Web site.
- Web browser: A program that displays Web pages by interpreting HTML code.
- WWW (World Wide Web): A type of Internet service that allows multimedia data programmed in HTML.

Credits

NETSCAPE
Courtesy of Netscape.

FIGURE 2-1
Courtesy of Dennis Anderson.

FIGURE 2-2
Courtesy of Dennis Anderson.

FIGURE 2-3
From navigators.com/internet_architecture.html by permission of Russ
Haynal—Internet Instructor, Speaker and Paradigm Shaker.
http://navigators.com.

FIGURE 2-4
From navigators.com/internet_architecture.html by permission of Russ
Haynal—Internet Instructor, Speaker and Paradigm Shaker.
http://navigators.com.

FIGURE 2-5
From navigators.com/internet_architecture.html by permission of Russ
Haynal—Internet Instructor, Speaker and Paradigm Shaker.
http://navigators.com.

FIGURE 2-6
From navigators.com/internet_architecture.html by permission of Russ
Haynal—Internet Instructor, Speaker and Paradigm Shaker.
http://navigators.com.

FIGURE 2-7
From navigators.com/internet_architecture.html by permission of Russ
Haynal—Internet Instructor, Speaker and Paradigm Shaker.
http://navigators.com.

FIGURE 2-8

From navigators.com/internet_architecture.html by permission of Russ Haynal—Internet Instructor, Speaker and Paradigm Shaker. http://navigators.com.

FIGURE 2-9

From navigators.com/internet_architecture.html by permission of Russ Haynal—Internet Instructor, Speaker and Paradigm Shaker. http://navigators.com.

FIGURE 2-10

From navigators.com/internet_architecture.html by permission of Russ Haynal—Internet Instructor, Speaker and Paradigm Shaker. http://navigators.com.

FIGURE 3-1

Reproduced with permission of Yahoo! Inc. c 2000 by Yahoo! Inc. YAHOO! and the YAHOO! logo are trademarks of Yahoo! Inc.

FIGURE 3-2

Courtesy of Robert I. Kabacoff, Ph.D.

FIGURE 3-3

Courtesy of Dennis Anderson.

FIGURE 3-4

Courtesy of Trinity College.

FIGURE 3-5

Example of packet switching in Japanese network.

FIGURE 3-6

Courtesy of Dennis Anderson.

FIGURE 3-7

Courtesy of Dennis Anderson.

FIGURE 3-8

From www.educ.drake.educ/rc/newsgroups.html.

FIGURE 3-9

Courtesy of Dennis Anderson.

FIGURE 4-1

Reproduced with permission of Yahoo! Inc. c 2000 by Yahoo! Inc. YAHOO! and the YAHOO! logo are trademarks of Yahoo! Inc.

FIGURE 4-2

Courtesy of AltaVista.

FIGURE 4-3

HotBot is a registered trademark and/or service mark of Wired Ventures, Inc. a Lycos Company. All rights reserved.

FIGURE 4-4

Courtesy of Switchboard Incorporated.

FIGURE 4-5
From www.theultimates.com/white. Reprinted by permission.

CHAPTER 5, P. 35
From hosmer.watertown.k12.ma.us/grade4science/index.html. Reprinted by permission of Vlad Baloh and the Hosmer School.

FIGURE 5-1
Image courtesy of the Franklin Insitute Science Museum.

FIGURE 5-2
From United States Department of Agriculture.

CHAPTER 5, P. 36
From United States Department of Agriculture.

FIGURE 5-3
From Nasa.

CHAPTER 5, P. 38
From Nasa.

CHAPTER 5, P. 38
From Nasa.

FIGURE 5-4
From btc.montana.edu/ceres/. Reprinted by permission of NASA/CERES (Center for Educational Resources) at Montana State University-Bozeman.

CHAPTER 5, P. 40
From btc.montana.edu/ceres/universe1/home.html. Reprinted by permission of NASA/CERES (Center for Educational Resources) at Montana State University-Bozeman.

FIGURE 5-5
From www.nyu.edu/projects/mstep/menu.html. Reprinted by permission of Pamela Fraser-Abder, Ph.D. Program Director, grant funded by the State Education Depart. Dwight D. Eisenhower program.

CHAPTER 5, P. 41
From www.nyu.edu/projects/mstep/lessons/aquatic.html. Reprinted by permission of Pamela Fraser-Abder, Ph.D. Program Director, grant funded by the State Education Depart. Dwight D. Eisenhower program.

FIGURE 5-6
Reprinted by permission.

CHAPTER 5, P. 42
Reprinted by permission.

FIGURE 5-7
Reprinted by permission of Math Forum and WebCT.

CHAPTER 5, P. 43
Reprinted by permission of Math Forum and WebCT.

CHAPTER 5, P. 43
Reprinted by permission of Math Forum and WebCT.

FIGURE 5-8
From www.nctm.org.

FIGURE 5-9
Courtesy of Annenberg/CPB.

FIGURE 5-10
Image courtesy Michael Trinklein.

FIGURE 5-11
Courtesy of the End of the Oregon Trail Interpretive Center, Oregon City, OR.

FIGURE 5-12
From www.emory.edu/carlos/odyssey/

CHAPTER 5, P. 46
From www.emory.edu/carlos/odyssey/egypt/homepg.html

FIGURE 5-13
From Library of Congress.

CHAPTER 5, P. 48
Courtesy of Center for the Liberal Arts, University of Virginia.

CHAPTER 5, P. 49
Reprinted by permission of Daniel C. Stevenson.

CHAPTER 5, P. 49
From U.S. Department of Education.

CHAPTER 5, P. 50
From Library of Congress

FIGURE 5-14
From www.utm.edu/departments/french/tflta.html. Reprinted by permission of The Tennessee Foreign Language Teaching Association and the page designer: Robert D. Peckham and the design organization: The Globe-Gate Project, University of Tennessee-Martin.

FIGURE 5-15
Reprinted by permission from www.itp.berkeley.edu/HumanResources.html.

FIGURE 5-16
Reprinted by permission of Iowa State University.

FIGURE 5-17
Reprinted with permission from www.aahperd.org. Copyright 2000 by

the American Alliance for Health, Physical Education, Recreation and Dance, 1900 Association Drive, Reston, VA 20191.

FIGURE 5-18
Used with permission from PE Central (www.pecentral.org), the premier Web site for Health and Physical Educators.

CHAPTER 5, P. 52
Used with permission from PE Central (www.pecentral.org), the premier Web site for Health and Physical Educators.

FIGURE 5-19
Guggenheim Museums webpage. www.guggenheim.org. c Solomon R. Guggenheim Foundation, New York. Reprinted by permission.

CHAPTER 5, P. 53
Clemente Exhibition webpage. www.guggenheim.org. c Solomon R. Guggenheim Foundation, New York. Reprinted by permission.

FIGURE 5-20
From www.moma.org.

CHAPTER 5, P. 54
From www.moma.org.

FIGURE 5-21
From United States Department of Education.

FIGURE 6-1
Microsoft FrontPage program.

FIGURE 6-2
Courtesy of Sausage Software.

FIGURE 6-3
Courtesy of Dennis Anderson.

FIGURE 6-4
Courtesy of Dennis Anderson.

FIGURE 6-5
Simple text editors.

FIGURE 6-6
Courtesy of Dennis Anderson.

FIGURE 6-7
Courtesy of Dennis Anderson.

FIGURE 6-8
Courtesy of Dennis Anderson.

FIGURE 6-9
Courtesy of Dennis Anderson.

FIGURE 6-10
Courtesy of Dennis Anderson.

FIGURE 6-11
Courtesy of Dennis Anderson.

FIGURE 6-12
Courtesy of Dennis Anderson.

FIGURE 6-13
Courtesy of Dennis Anderson.

FIGURE 6-14
Courtesy of Dennis Anderson.

FIGURE 6-15
Courtesy of Dennis Anderson.

FIGURE 6-16
Courtesy of Dennis Anderson.

FIGURE 6-17
Courtesy of Dennis Anderson.

FIGURE 6-18
Courtesy of Dennis Anderson.

FIGURE 6-19
Courtesy of Dennis Anderson.

FIGURE 6-20
Courtesy of Dennis Anderson.

FIGURE 6-21
Courtesy of Dennis Anderson.

FIGURE 6-22
Courtesy of Dennis Anderson.

FIGURE 6-23
Adapted from Reza's HTML color guide, Drexel Univ, 1998.

FIGURE 6-24
Courtesy of Dennis Anderson.

FIGURE 6-25
Courtesy of Dennis Anderson.

FIGURE 6-26
Courtesy of Dennis Anderson.

FIGURE 6-27
Courtesy of Dennis Anderson.

FIGURE 6-28
Courtesy of Dennis Anderson.

FIGURE 6-29
Courtesy of Dennis Anderson.

FIGURE 6-30
Courtesy of Dennis Anderson.

FIGURE 6-31
Courtesy of Dennis Anderson.

FIGURE 6-32
Courtesy of Dennis Anderson.

FIGURE 6-33
Courtesy of Dennis Anderson.

FIGURE 6-34
Courtesy of Dennis Anderson.

FIGURE 6-35, P. 80
Courtesy of Dennis Anderson.

FIGURE 6-36
Courtesy of Dennis Anderson.

FIGURE 6-37
Courtesy of Dennis Anderson.

FIGURE 6-38
Courtesy of Dennis Anderson.

FIGURE 6-39
Courtesy of Dennis Anderson.

FIGURE 6-40
Courtesy of Dennis Anderson.

FIGURE 6-41
Courtesy of Dennis Anderson.

FIGURE 6-42
Telnet program.

FIGURE 7-1
Courtesy of Dennis Anderson.

FIGURE 7-2
From www.lib.utexas.edu/libs/pcl/map_collection/map_sites/map_sites.html

FIGURE 7-3
Copyrighted by Merriam-Webster Inc. Reprinted with permission from the publisher. For additional language information visit Merriam-Webster OnLine at www.merriam-webster.com.

FIGURE 7-4
Courtesy of AltaVista.

FIGURE 7-5

From www.math.sc.edu/~sumner/. Reprinted by permission.

FIGURE 7-6

c 2000 Manhattan Transfer. Reprinted by permission.

FIGURE 7-7

Courtesy ChatSpace, Inc.